Faith in Europe

Faith in Europe?

The Cardinal's Lectures

A series of six public lectures at Westminster Cathedral

Jean Vanier
Mary McAleese
Timothy Radcliffe OP
Bob Geldof
Chris Patten
Cormac Murphy-O'Connor

DARTON·LONGMAN + TODD

First published in 2005 by
Darton, Longman and Todd Ltd
1 Spencer Court
140–142 Wandsworth High Street
London
SW18 4JJ

ISBN 0 232 52630 3

A catalogue record for this book is available from the British
Library.

Phototypeset by IntypeLibra Ltd, London
Printed and bound in Great Britain by
Page Bros, Norwich, Norfolk

Contents

The Lecturers

Jean Vanier established the first l'Arche community in 1964; now there are over 100 communities in thirty countries where people with learning disabilities and their assistants live and work together as equals. His many books include *Drawn into the Mystery of Jesus through the Gospel of John* and *Befriending the Stranger*.

Mary McAleese, a former Professor of Law at Trinity College Dublin and Pro-Vice Chancellor of the Queen's University of Belfast, was inaugurated as the eighth President of Ireland in 1997.

Timothy Radcliffe OP is an itinerant preacher and lecturer based at Blackfriars, Oxford. He was Master of the Dominican Order between 1992 and 2001. His books include *Sing a New Song, I Call You Friends* and *Just One Year*.

Bob Geldof is a musician who helped found the band The Boomtown Rats. In 1985 he organised the Live Aid charity concert, raising over £50 million. In 2005, he organised the Live 8 concert in order to raise awareness of third world poverty which was then under discussion at the G8 Summit. He has been awarded an honorary KBE for his humanitarian work.

Lord Patten of Barnes CH was Governor of Hong Kong from 1992 to 1997, and a European Commissioner between 1999 and 2004. He is Chancellor of Newcastle University and Oxford University. He is the author of *East and West* and, most recently, *Not Quite the Diplomat: Home Truths About World Affairs*.

Cardinal Cormac Murphy-O'Connor was the Rector of the English College, Rome, from 1972 to 1977, when he became the Bishop of Arundel and Brighton. He was installed as the tenth Archbishop of Westminster in 2000 and was created a cardinal by Pope John Paul II the following year.

Introduction

The *Faith in Europe?* lectures held at Westminster Cathedral in April-May 2005 were, as it turned out, providentially timed. We could not have known, when we planned the series back in 2003, that the lectures would coincide with a papal interregnum and a crisis of identity in the European Union.

The inspiration for the series was Pope John Paul II's magnificent post-synodal apostolic exhortation on Europe, *Ecclesia in Europa*, which was issued in June 2003. In it John Paul II called for Europeans to 'relive their roots', to recognise their true identity; he wanted us to take stock, to be more authentically ourselves. It struck me, when I read his words, that in Britain we find it hard to use such language of Europe, let alone to see it as a culture with a soul.

John Paul II was not offering a view of the single currency, or of a European central bank. *Ecclesia in Europa* is silent on agricultural subsidies.

His idea was that Europe — a much larger, and more ancient, territory than the contemporary European Union — has a mission to the world: a vocation, if you will. Seen through the prism of our endless debates over Britain's place in Europe this can sound to British ears like a sort of spiritual version of the papers put out by Brussels. And that is the difficulty. The British people have for so long viewed Europe through the lenses of politics and economics that a larger perspective requires, as it were, new spectacles. The six speakers who made up the *Faith in Europe?* series offered that new vision.

Jean Vanier, the founder of the l'Arche communities, spoke just after the funeral of John Paul II, while I was still in Rome; but word soon reached me that he had given the kind of talk which over years has enabled many people to confront what it is to be human, in all our fragility and dignity. How essential it is for Europe to accept the 'primacy of the human', and not that of money, say, or youth, or success, Vanier argued. He has shown this so vividly in his prophetic communities: how it is the vulnerable who have most to teach Europe about what it means to be human. It is in our response to vulnerability that our continent will be judged. Belonging, loving, accepting our brokenness – can these be the hallmarks of European culture?

A Europe of reconciliation is what Mary McAleese invited us to build. And she is careful to remind us that such reconciliation is forged by treaties and covenants and consensus-building. She points to the ideals at the origin of the European Union and sees them as all of a piece with Europe's wider vocation. She reminded us from where we have come: in the debris of post-war Europe, she said, 'a group of men and women consciously decided to try love and not hate'. That is a profound calling, which Europe must not forget.

When we speak of the role of faith in Europe, it is all too easy to think of stone crosses and vast cathedrals, to imagine the Church as an institution with an ancient history. But Fr Timothy Radcliffe looks beyond, to the pilgrim paths that continue to cross the continent alongside its motorways and railtracks. Searching is his theme. The popularity of pilgrimages suggests, he says, 'that there is something to be sought', and more so now, in this age of collapsing grand narratives. People are suspicious of grand truth claims; the task of Christianity, says Timothy Radcliffe, is now 'to remind Europeans of our buried desire for the truth, and walk with them as they search'. Beauty, truth and goodness are the lodestars; will Europe let them shine?

Europe's vocation to the wider world is the theme tackled by both Sir Bob Geldof and Lord Patten, but in quite different ways. Geldof's oratory held a packed cathedral in thrall; many might have come to hear his at times colourful language, but they left ready to follow him to the G8 Summit in Edinburgh. Geldof by turns shamed and cajoled Europe, demanding that we keep before our eyes the plight of Africa, insisting that a suburban, pusillanimous Europe is not worthy of its name. How great Europe will be, he suggests, when it exists not for itself but for the poorest.

Lord Patten, on the other hand, concerned himself with the question of Europe's borders – why they need to keep pushing back to enable struggling nations to enter into partnerships of solidarity and democracy. 'A stable and democratic neighbourhood, support for the international rule of law and the institutions that seek to monitor it, and the pursuit of external values in external policy' – these are, for Lord Patten, the traits of a Europe with a mission to the world.

Pope John Paul II observed in *Ecclesia in Europa* that our continent has 'a growing need of hope, a hope that will enable us to give meaning to life and history, and to continue on our way together'. Hope, meaning and purpose: these are what Europe needs to offer. That means we must draw deep from the wellsprings, and acknowledge our destiny. We need to think bigger and more boldly. We need to have faith in our continent, just as God surely does. I hope these reflections will help to build that faith – and a better future for Europe.

1 Hope in Europe: Becoming More Human

Jean Vanier

I find it very moving to be here to talk about 'Hope in Europe' shortly after the death of our beloved Pope John Paul II. Because the funeral and the whole of the reality around it was an incredible sign of hope. And I believe that we are called to look deeply into the legacy of John Paul II because he leaves an immense legacy of holiness and an incredible legacy after these last years where he became particularly fragile, vulnerable and poor. I think that those years, when he was barely able to talk or to walk, were greater than any encyclical. It is the good shepherd who gives his life for the flock. There are two particular elements, I believe, that are part of the vision, part of the incredible vision of John Paul II: two elements that were particularly wounding to his heart. One was the growing gap between rich and poor, between rich countries and poor countries. The other element was his cry for peace, to break down the dividing wall that separates countries, groups and so on. On one side his cry for compassion, which says something about the lessening of the gap between the rich and the poor. On the other side forgiveness. One of the strong words that he used was that there can be no peace without justice, and no justice without forgiveness.

From a divided Europe to a united Europe

In May/June 1940 I was eleven years old, and a refugee, with my family, fleeing the north of France invaded by the Nazi army. Since my father was in the diplomatic corps, we were able to escape in a British destroyer which brought us to a cargo ship, the *Nariva*, and then to England. In 1942, I joined the Royal Naval College in Dartmouth.

1

JEAN VANIER

In January 1944, a few months after the liberation of Paris, I accompanied my mother who was in the Canadian Red Cross, to the Gare d'Orsay in Paris – the train station where hundreds of men and women arrived like skeletons in their striped blue and white uniforms, from Dachau, Buchenwald, Ravensbrück and other concentration camps. So, as an adolescent and young adult I was caught up in the things of war.

War is a horrible reality.

We can give thanks for men like Schuman, Adenauer, De Gasperi and many others who laid the foundations for a united Europe where conflicts could be resolved and where people of different cultures could meet.

* * *

Europe today can, and hopefully will, become an even more wonderful meeting place or training ground, a school of mutual acceptance, a human laboratory not just for the resolution of conflict but also for the discovery of the beauty of different cultures, different peoples.

France, for example, is not just a place for good wine and cheese and football teams! It is a land of beautiful cathedrals, old Roman and Gothic churches; Italy is a land of Giotto, Piero della Francesca, Dante, Francis of Assisi. As we begin to learn each other's language, as we visit each other's country and discover each other's culture, we can begin to open up to a wonderful and deep sense of our common humanity. We begin to meet people, each person hidden behind the label of nationality or culture.

But even more: we can join together with our wealth, competence and wisdom to make of our world – not just Europe – a better place. Young people of different countries can come together and discover the joy of service, particularly to those in serious need in Europe and other continents.

The primacy of the person

Over the last centuries, European countries were at war with each other. There was fear, hatred and suspicion between them. Different Christian Churches were

2

estranged from each other, even fought each other. The so-called upper classes and lower classes did not meet. There were clubs for some and bars for others. Men knew that they were better than women!

The colour bar and racism rampant in the United States was also strong in many countries of Europe. Forms of slavery existed in order to have cheaper labour. People were defined by their group. Each group had a more or less closed identity. People knew who was right and who was wrong, who was good and who was bad.

Since the beginning of the twentieth century, particularly since 1950, an immense revolution or evolution is taking place. From the primacy of the group, the tribe or the country there has grown an awareness of the primacy of the person: the value, importance and beauty of each person. This has come about through:

- a sense of the horror of war, genocide, particularly the Shoah
- the creation of the United Nations, the proclamation of human rights, the protection of minority groups
- our multi-cultural, pluralistic societies where people of different cultures and origins work together
- the development and growth of psychotherapy and other forms of therapy that help people discover their person and their real needs, hidden behind the knots of their story
- the insistence of Christian churches on the person loved by God and called by God.

These factors — plus many others — have led people to a new type of relationship, particularly with those who are 'different'.

People of different Christian churches and different religions are meeting, respecting one another. There are places of dialogue.

People with disabilities or with mental illness are seen as fully human beings.

Each person is being called to develop his or her personal conscience.

The gifts, wisdom and beauty of people coming from different African and Asian cultures are being recognised.

When the person is sought underneath the label, the

world is no longer divided into the good and the bad, one group superior to others.

People realise that the 'good' and the 'bad' are in each one of us, in you, in me, in all of us. It takes a lifetime for all the light to emerge from the darkness within each one of us.

But there is another side of the story

In our societies today, it is not always the primacy of the person that has emerged: a strong self-centredness has also been unleashed. With the breakdown of social and religious restraints, many people use their freedom for their own material success, egotistical pleasure, sexual activity without any commitment or sense of responsibility for others. This individualism can lead some people to loneliness and a feeling of emptiness, which in turn can push them to seek closed sectarian political and religious groups which give security, a sense of superiority which can enhance group conflicts. Once again the world can be divided into the 'good' and the 'bad'.

The primacy of the person implies a belief in the sacredness and interiority of each person, with his/her gifts, his/her brokenness and in all his/her differences. It brings people to love and to be responsible. It does not use others nor seek to possess or control them. It respects what is most precious in each person and seeks to help each one rediscover his/her dignity and self-esteem. The social and theological vision of John Paul II is based upon this truth: the importance of each person, each one created by God and for God; each one has his/her inner conscience and is capable of welcoming God, becoming the dwelling place of God. Etty Hillesum was a young Dutch Jewish woman who was assassinated in Auschwitz in November 1943. In one of her letters from Westerbork, the camp where some 10,000 Jews were waiting to be carted off to Auschwitz, she wrote:

> And I thank You for the great gift of being able to read people. Sometimes they seem to me like houses with open doors... every one must be turned into a dwelling place for You, O God.

And I promise You, yes, I promise that I shall try to find a dwelling and a refuge for You in as many houses as possible. There are so many empty houses, and I shall prepare them all for You, the most honoured Guest. Please forgive this poor metaphor.

Let us hope that with Europe as a 'laboratory' and a meeting place for people with those who are 'different', a new and deeper vision of the person and of human freedom may grow.

But we have to admit that this discovery of the value of each person is a long road where we are confronted by all the pressures of the media and the surrounding culture of pleasure, and material success, and by our own inner fragility and poverty.

Our human fragility

As we look at ourselves and at our world, we have to admit that we human beings are a broken and wounded people. It is moving to see, in the book of Genesis, the first words of Adam after he had turned away from God. He responded to God who was looking for him:

'I was frightened
because I was naked
and I hid.' (Gen. 3:10)

At the heart of each one of us, descendants of Adam, there is the same terrible sense of 'nakedness', inner poverty and emptiness that often frightens us and makes us hide from God and from others. Who are we? What is the meaning of our lives? We seek to *be someone*, by comparing ourselves to others; we have to be better, stronger, more clever, than them. If we are not better than others, then we become depressed and sad, victims. We are all frightened of showing our brokenness and poverty.

With Adam and Eve's broken relationship and broken communion with God, competition, hatred, oppression, contempt, jealousy, violence entered into the world. Cain killed his brother Abel. To control this violence, strong, closed groups were created with their rituals, laws and

5

powerful authority. Violence was contained in the group but individual freedom was curtailed if not crushed.

Conflict then broke out between groups, cultures and religions. Each group had to show that it was more powerful than the others. To be a warrior, to die for one's country, was noble.

Does this mean that the culture and religion which formed these groups were just for personal security and protection against the emptiness and the loneliness of individuals?

Culture, religion and the emergence of the 'I'

Religion, morality and culture *can* become walls behind which people can hide their nakedness and their fear of relationships. They feel secure, superior, powerful behind them.

But religious traditions and cultures can also become the roots of our human growth in maturity and spirituality. They give us the necessary inner security to enable us to go beyond that which separates us from others, to meet those who are different, to discover their beauty and value, to serve and love them. To discover also that we are all part of an immense human family, that each person is important for God.

Jesus came not to destroy the different ways that lead to God and to truth, but to fulfil them, to confirm them – even to go deeper – to lead each person into a new meeting with God, a communion with God.

My hope is that we may learn to cherish – and even more to love deeply – our own Church, our own religion and our own culture because they can open us up to a greater love of our own person, to God, to truth, to life and to love those who are different. They can call us to a greater maturity, while deeply respecting others and seeing the work of God within them.

I believe that the genius of John Paul was, on the one hand, to affirm and deepen the identity of Catholics and, on the other, to open us up to others who are different, to meet them, love, respect and understand them. Was that not his vision as he called leaders of different churches and religions to Assisi in 1986 and in 2002?

Small communities

How can we seek to live the primacy of the person and yet belong to a specific Church or a religion that proclaims an absolute?

How can we pass from a vision of the world, where it is clear who is bad and who is good, who is wrong and who is right, what is false and what is true . . . to an awareness that both the bad and the good, the wrong and the right are in you, in me, in each one of us?

My experience is that we cannot truly discover the person of another community and respect and appreciate him or her with all that is negative and positive, without a place of belonging where we are bonded together with others, can share together our joys and pains, and help each other to grow to greater wisdom and maturity.

The first community is the family where man and woman – after a honeymoon period and a delightful and exciting fusion – discover how different they are! Family life – with the children that are given – is a long road towards acceptance of the other, admiring and rejoicing in their gifts, being patient with their faults and inadequacies, learning day after day to forgive. Today for many reasons, the family is in danger. Breakdowns in communication can arise quickly. Children who do not have the privilege of a happy family bonding need other places of belonging.

These places of belonging are not formed only by people with a common goal. They are places of mutual caring and covenant relationships. They are like schools where people learn to relate, to love others as they are, to meet the person behind the label, to live tenderness, to communicate, to forgive, to work together, to grow in inner freedom, and to learn to disarm their need to be right and to control.

They are places where people can learn about themselves, learn to welcome their own personal story and accept their shadow side. They become more conscious of their fears, their nakedness and their need to hide. It is there that they learn to come out from behind their hiding places and begin to grow to greater personal maturity, freedom, wholeness and wisdom.

These places of belonging need, however, to be open, leading each person to greater freedom, giving the opportunity for some to leave, if it is good for their growth. Small, open communities are essential to help people come out of the pangs of emptiness, loneliness, anguish and insecurity, and yet not fall into the closed, fearful sectarian groups which bring apparent security but crush a sense of freedom.

My experience of forty years of living with people with disabilities in small communities of celebration

The power of an intelligent and tender love

For a long time before 1960, across Europe, hundreds and hundreds of dismal, often overcrowded institutions and hospitals were filled with terribly lonely children and adults with disabilities who had been 'put aside'.

Some parents, horribly disappointed and surprised by the birth of a child with disabilities, felt guilty; they saw no meaning to their child and felt obliged to put him or her away. These children and adults were often considered 'not fully human', not fully a person, nonentities, a mistake or an error of nature. Our Churches frequently ignored their importance as children of God.

What have we, in l'Arche and in Faith and Light, discovered? Hidden underneath the label of disability, there is a person yearning for relationship.

Did you know that it was only in the 1930s that Dr Bowlby and others like him discovered the value and importance of parental love – made of tenderness, attentiveness – for the growth of the child towards maturity?

A person who was not loved as a child or a person who has been physically or sexually abused as a child and has lived in the shadow of fear, will have more difficulty growing into a mature, free human being. They have to protect their extreme vulnerability. If a child is not loved, will he or she be able to grow in love? If a child is not seen and

8

respected as a person how will he or she learn to see and respect others as persons?

To love is not to possess or to control another. To love is to respect another.

To love is to reveal to another person their value and beauty; to help them rediscover their self-esteem, deepen their personal conscience and become more fully themselves and not just what others want them to be.

In the 130 l'Arche communities and the 1,500 Faith and Light communities around the world, we have witnessed the incredible power of intelligent love. Children and adults who had been considered only as 'a problem', a source of pain and distress, considered as having no value, no dignity, tend to close up in anger, and depression and sometimes self-mutilation. Or else they will flee into a world of dreams or madness.

If they live in a community where they are loved and respected and where they receive help in order to develop humanly and spiritually, they flourish and become more fully themselves. The disability as such may not be cured, but they can open up to their environment and to others and learn to live with their limits and handicaps in a deeply human way.

What is amazing for many of us in l'Arche is not so much the peace and joy and growth in spiritual and human capacities of people with disabilities, but the growth of young people – and less young – who come and share their lives with them, who often say that through this shared life they themselves have been transformed; they have discovered a new meaning to their lives.

Let me tell you the story of a thirty-year-old woman who claims she was transformed by her shared life in l'Arche. She had grown up fearing relationships, hiding from them, because her parents were always quarrelling. Relationships for her were seen as dangerous. She decided to work hard in her studies and at work and she did well. She was promoted and was a success. She admitted, however, that she was wearing a mask, protecting herself, her vulnerability, and her own heart and affectivity. She discovered l'Arche almost by mistake and her whole world has changed. She discovered living, loving, kind and tender relationships;

person-to-person, heart-to-heart relationships. She realised that people loved and appreciated her but did not seek to possess or control her. The people with learning disabilities she lived with were not caught up in a world of politeness and social conventions. They were not struggling for power or seeking to prove they were better than others; they were simple and open. They awoke her own heart and helped her to discover who she really was. She discovered with them the communion of hearts and a way to come out from behind her hiding places.

* * *

Sometimes I go to the restaurant with Gerard. In the middle of the meal he gets up and goes over to people at the other tables to say, 'Hello, I'm Gerard. What is your name?' He has a deep sense of our common humanity!

People like Gerard are 'people for people', they live for relationships; they are not people seeking a place in the hierarchy of power.

The importance of the person

The main aspect of our life in community is that we are centred around the well-being of each person, particularly those who are the weakest. Many in l'Arche cannot talk and we need to learn to understand their body language: their smiles, their anger, their violence, their tenderness in order to understand them and help them to discover their beauty and to grow.

What is important is 'you', your development, your bodily welfare, your needs, your happiness, your place, how you can grow humanly and spiritually. You are more important than the community! All that obviously takes time, a lot of listening and often good professional help.

L'Arche is founded on the need for an intelligent, wise love, so that each person may discover who he or she is and grow to greater maturity.

Love is at the heart of the Christian message.

The values of our European culture are justice and respect for people. We are all called to seek the common good, help in the creation of good laws, work for justice and truth, and develop centres of education where human values are seen as essential, where young people are taught to work together, to co-operate and to understand those who are different.

Compassion and forgiveness

But as followers of Jesus we are called to go further than justice and the creation of good laws, and discover two particular virtues and attitudes which are essential if we are to work for peace: compassion and forgiveness.

Compassion and forgiveness always go hand in hand. Jesus brings them together when he says:

> 'Be compassionate
> as my Father is compassionate.
> Do not judge or condemn
> but forgive.' (Luke 6:36)

Compassion seeks to lessen the gap between the powerful and the powerless, the rich and the poor. Forgiveness seeks to bring down the walls and frontiers that separate people who reject each other, who refuse to speak to each other.

Structures cannot be compassionate or forgiving, not even a community can be compassionate. It can encourage people to be compassionate, but as such a community is governed by rules, or laws and a constitution that specifies its goals and form of government. Only a person, a human heart, touched by the pain of another, can be compassionate and inspire the adequate response to pain.

Compassion is lived when each one of us bends down and welcomes the person who is lonely, lost and in need, the one who has lost self-esteem, is confused, depressed or angry.

It is not simply to give something to people who are economically poor. It is first of all to reveal to a person that he or she has value, is important and unique and can grow and do beautiful things. It is to help each one to help themselves and find meaning to their lives.

This revelation is not always easy to transmit when people are locked up in fear and self-hate or when they have lost self-esteem. It takes time, a deep love, the wisdom

11

of relationships, and often professional expertise to help them open up and discover who they are.

Here I would like to make a distinction between generosity and communion of heart.

Those who are generous give from their wealth and knowledge to people in need; they bend down as those who are superior to those who are inferior, as those who *have* to those who *have not*, the rich give to the poor. They are in control of the situation and give what they want and when they want.

Generosity hopefully will flow into a communion of hearts where we meet those who are weaker as people; we listen to their story and our hearts are touched. We no longer seek to control them or to show them that we are superior; we become their friend. The gap that separated us has been reduced. We have become vulnerable one to the other.

Through this bonding or communion of hearts we not only give but we also receive; we give life and receive life. We help people to rise up and rediscover their self-esteem. They have a friend who trusts in them, so they too can grow in trust.

Compassion then is healing for the one who receives compassion but also for the one who gives compassion. Both persons are transformed; both discover their true personhood.

When a mother has lost her son in an accident, there is not much we can do. What she needs is someone to be with her, who lives a communion of hearts with her.

Compassion implies wisdom: do not dive into the sea to save a drowning person unless you have a rope you can hang on to! That rope is wisdom. We must not sink into the suffering of others but help the suffering person to find life and meaning.

Compassion implies that: we see the person behind the label of difference, pain, sickness or weakness and move from a sense of superiority and power to a relationship of friendship and mutual vulnerability.

As we seek to be compassionate for the one who is lost, lonely and in pain, we learn to become compassionate for our own selves, for the broken one within us that we have hidden away behind a mask and that we do not want to see. But how to die to this deep psychological need to prove that we are better than others? Here let me quote a prayer of the Patriarch Athenagoras of Constantinople:

> I have waged this war against myself for many years.
> It was terrible.
> But now I am disarmed.
> I am no longer frightened of anything because love banishes fear.
> I am disarmed of the need to be right and to justify myself by disqualifying others.
> I am no longer on the defensive, holding onto my riches.

I still have a long way to go to be disarmed. I have touched and experienced the anger, violence and emptiness within my own self and have become more aware that the anguish and feeling of helplessness are not something that I can conquer through my own will and efforts. To become I need the compassionate power of the Holy Spirit to come into the places of my own darkness, loneliness and emptiness, into those places of pain I am hiding away, and reveal to me that I am precious to God, loved by God, just as I am, in all my brokenness. I don't have to be better than others.

Let me reflect with you on one of the most powerful parables of Jesus, the parable of the Good Samaritan.

This story is about two people who belong to two hostile groups, which had been enemies for hundreds of years. The story takes place in six acts:

- A Jewish man is beaten by robbers and left lying on the road.
- Three men of the same religious tradition see him lying there and refuse to stop. Why? Fear. Fear of what? Why don't we stop?
- A man of another culture, a 'Samaritan', an enemy of the Jewish people of that time, sees the Jewish man lying on the ground and stops. He sees in this wounded Jewish man a brother in humanity.
- He knows what to do. He is competent and tender. He pours wine and oil on the wounds and helps the wounded man to get onto his donkey. Competence and tenderness are two essential ingredients of compassion.

13

- He spends the night with him and becomes his friend. He moves from an attitude of generosity to a communion of hearts.
- He leaves humbly, in the morning, asking nothing in return.

At the end of this parable Jesus says: 'Go and do likewise.' How difficult it is to 'do likewise'!

Can we do it without the help of the Paraclete, the Holy Spirit? Can we be compassionate to the broken and the lonely if our hearts of stone have not been transformed into hearts of flesh, if we are still concerned about our own superiority?

Forgiveness is at the heart of the Christian message and at the heart of every human relationship.

> There is no peace without justice,
> No justice without forgiveness. (John Paul II)

Isn't our daily prayer: 'Forgive us our trespasses as we forgive those who trespass against us'?

Guilt is in all of us. We have hurt others and have been hurt by others. Walls have risen up between us. We need to be liberated from this guilt by the power of forgiveness.

We need to liberate others through the power of our forgiveness.

We need to be forgiven by the lonely, the weak, the rejected, the poor, the lost with whom we have not shared our wealth, our time, our hearts.

We need to be forgiven by other cultures, churches, religions that we have not respected, from whom we have turned away, with a feeling of superiority.

Forgiveness is not just 'let's forget past hurts'. It is seeing the person of the one we called the enemy behind the label.

It is the transformation of conflict into friendship, seeing the other, loving him or her as Jesus sees and loves him or her.

This means that we have become aware of all that is dead within us, that we were and are a source of death for others because of our prejudices, our indifference and sometimes our hatred. Can we forgive others if we are not aware of how much we need to be forgiven?

Last June at a Festival for Peace in Northern Ireland, I listened to the testimony of Aaron, from Israel. His youngest son was in the army and was killed by a Hamas group in Southern Lebanon. His eldest son became mentally ill because of his younger brother's death and by things he had seen done by the brutality of the army in Gaza. Instead of closing up in anger, depression and a desire for vengeance, Aaron met with another Israeli father whose two sons had also been killed in the war. These two grieving fathers made contact with Palestinian families whose sons had been killed. Together they founded 'Families for Peace'.

In the face of intense suffering we can rise up and become peacemakers.

In a Europe which seeks to be a place of peace and a source of peace, we all need to take the road of forgiveness. But it is a long road. What will jolt us out of our need for comfort and security, and give us the strength to be peacemakers?

Forgiveness, like compassion, is impossible on a purely human level. Jesus calls us to love our enemies, to do good to those who hate us, to speak well of those who speak badly of us, to pray for those who crush us. Isn't that love impossible? To bend down to those who are lost and lonely, and to become their friend. Isn't that impossible?

Compassion and forgiveness become possible through the presence of Jesus: He is the Prince of Peace.

> 'If you love me and keep my word
> I will pray the Father
> and he will send you another Paraclete
> to be with you forever...' (John 14:15-16)

Yes, the Paraclete will be with us forever to reduce the gap between the powerful and the powerless, between the rich and the poor, not only through good legislation but through personal encounters with people, listening to their stories, heart to heart. The Paraclete will be with us to open cracks in the walls that separate us from enemies and from those we dislike. The Paraclete will change our hearts of stone into hearts of flesh; and will soften our hearts. We will discover a new love, an intelligent love that opens us up and helps us to discover a new and deeper fraternity and bonding.

My hope is that our very emptiness, our nakedness, can become a cry to the God who became flesh, who descended with compassion from his place of superiority, to look for us and to meet us, in all our brokenness, lostness and nakedness. He can fill our emptiness with his presence. This emptiness no longer needs to remain hidden; it becomes the very place where we call on God and meet God in a new way.

Jesus is knocking at the door of our hearts, waiting for us to open so that he may dwell in us, and we in him, so that he may make of us men and women of compassion and forgiveness.

Etty Hillesum, in all the pain and horror she experienced in the Westerbork camp, prayed to God: 'You cannot help us but we must help You and defend Your dwelling place inside us'. God needs us to unlock the doors behind which we hide, to let God in, so that we may become men and women of compassion and forgiveness.

* * *

There are immense forces in our societies that tend to exalt power, physical strength and beauty. These economic, military and political powers use all forms of communication and psychological methods to impose a vision which incites people to seek power for their own glory, to seek rampant and greedy individualism, which crushes the weak and the vulnerable and even annihilates them.

In front of these huge forces, there are trickles of peacemakers.

My hope is that more and more men and women from different Christian Churches and different religions and different philosophies of life will rise up from what can seem to be for some the ruins of morality and religion, from the ruins also of rivalry, competition and economic domination, in order to serve those who are weak and vulnerable and be present to them. Every gesture of compassion, every act of forgiveness makes each one of us more human and brings us closer to God.

The training ground of Europe can then become the land of a new vision for peace in our world where we can discover that it is often the poor and the weak and minority groups who inspire us to become more human; who call forth what is deepest in us – goodness and compassion and who help us to discover what it means to be truly human and a friend of God.

That is my hope for Europe – not only for Europe, but also for the world.

2 Growing Up in Europe

Mary McAleese

Introduction

When I was growing up in Belfast one of the most dismissive things you could say to someone else or have said to you was, 'Oh, for God's sake, grow up!' So Cardinal Murphy O'Connor's invitation to give a talk entitled 'Growing Up in Europe' as part of a series with the theme 'Faith in Europe' had a tantalising and ambiguous edge to it which I look forward to exploring with you for the next hour or so. What does 'growing up' mean in a political context? Is it about us growing up, or Europe growing up, or both?

Of course, I made the mistake of saying 'yes' to the Cardinal's invitation and he then had to go to the bother of organising a Vatican Conclave so that he would have the best of excuses to avoid having to listen to tonight's lecture. His efforts failed. We welcome him home and offer to Pope Benedict XVI our good wishes and prayers.

The Catholic Church has been through an emotional time with the illness and death of Pope John Paul II and the overwhelming outpouring of sadness and affection which came from around the world and from every faith and perspective. I had the honour to lead the Irish delegation at the funeral of the Pope and to sit among representatives of many nations, some of whom have serious, unresolved problems with one another. They streamed to Rome to pay respect to a man who had paid respect to them and, while no treaties were signed that day, nor conflicts ended, there was at least a new bridge to each other of that one, shared memory and in that memory there lingers a flicker of hope for our chaotic humanity. With such diversity and so many people present in Rome it could have been chaos, but because the gathering came in love for John Paul, if not for each other, there was a noble civility about it, like a squabbling and estranged family gathered around the deathbed of a loving father, in whose love for them they might possibly find the spark of a rekindled love for each other. This coming together of the nations and the religions was not only a tribute to John Paul II's conduct of his ministry, it was in keeping with the vision of the Second Vatican Council. The first paragraph of *Lumen Gentium* ('The Light of the Nations'), describes the Church as a 'sacrament of unity among all men'. Let us pray this evening that the successor of John Paul II will use his powerful ministry to further the cause of Christian and human unity and respect for diversity. He will need our prayers – never have the shoes of the fisherman looked so large.

Summary in three main points

I have cited the documents of the Second Vatican Council and the life and work of John Paul II as an introduction to my reflections this evening, not simply because of the contemporary news focus on them, but because there is in them a point of reference and a source of encouragement for the things I want to say. I will pursue three lines of argument.

First, we should give ourselves credit for what has been achieved in Europe – for the Europe of Reconciliation that has emerged since the Second World War. As I said when I addressed the European Parliament eighteen months ago, 'If the war graves of Europe could speak they would tell us we are living a miracle.'

Second, the Europe of Reconciliation is not an isolated historical development. It forms part of a worldwide trajectory towards a different political culture where democracy and human rights are embedded and the dignity of the individual asserted and vindicated.

Third, the Europe we want to see is in an early stage of development. No one has given us a guarantee for the future. I will suggest some elements of risk that we need to bear in mind as we travel into that future.

As I embark on the wonderful privilege of addressing a great audience in a famous cathedral, my mind goes back to a short story by P.G. Wodehouse called 'The Great

19

Sermon Handicap'. The story is about young men who are placing bets on the length of the sermons in all the local churches. It's certainly one way of garnering youthful interest in church attendance and, for any of you who are up to the same tricks, I can assure you that I have not discussed race-fixing with Jean Vanier, Bob Geldof, Timothy Radcliffe or Chris Patten!

The Europe of Reconciliation

The question of Europe requires of us a number of important judgements.

Is the coming together of the nations of Europe a random thing, dictated by self-interest and money? Is it just one more phase in an endless cycle marked by the rise and fall of great powers? Or is there a valid view according to which European reconciliation should be seen as having a particular significance – as providential? Should the European Union be understood as a kind of growing up?

Underlying these questions are even more basic questions about political life. Does history have a purpose? Are we justified in seeking a pattern of meaning in our political history?

I have accepted this invitation because I do see a very particular significance in European unity and reconciliation. For the vast majority of Europeans, to be born in today's Europe, the Europe of 2005, offers the opportunity of a fuller self-understanding and much better prospects than to have been born in 1905, or when I was born in 1951, just after two appalling world wars which robbed millions of youngsters of the chance to grow up at all and cast long shadows of unfathomable sorrow over those who survived. In the last half-century, new political parameters have been defined and forces of reconciliation have been set free by the European Union, the Council of Europe and the Organisation for Security and Co-operation in Europe. Since the fall of the Berlin Wall, we have witnessed the beginning of the end of cultural divisions that have manifested themselves in different ways ever since the Romans drew their frontier along the Rhine and the Danube. Our habits, assumptions and expectations are quite different to the habits, assumptions and expectations of a hundred years ago or even twenty years ago, so rapid is the pace of change. Ireland is, of course, a famous example of a country that has been changed for the better by our membership of the European Union. The Union underpins all the other factors that have contributed to our economic revival. The values and institutions of the European Union have contributed to the framework for peace represented by the Good Friday Agreement. History will show that the first attempt at a settlement in Northern Ireland, between 1972 and 1973, coincided with Britain and Ireland 'entering Europe'. Our self-confidence, our music and our literature, the very face of our society – all have been transformed by the reconnection of Ireland to Europe.

Of course, each member state has its own story to tell. France and Germany have overcome one of the most damaging rivalries in history and in doing so have set an example to the world. For Spain, Greece and Portugal, Europe was a factor in the ending of dictatorships. For the new member states from Eastern Europe, the homecoming has been as remarkable as for Ireland. What a tremendous thing it is, in the light of history, for people to set out from Poland in their hundreds of thousands for the Pope's funeral, cross frontiers without impediment, and find a warm welcome in the streets and squares of the Eternal City! For Italy, the signing ceremony of the European Constitution and the funeral of John Paul II prove that even after two thousand years, all roads lead to Rome!

I see these changes not as chance occurrences but as the result of leadership given and choices made. Yes, we do seek to live by different values than in the past. Yes, we do propose a different 'anthropology' – a different understanding of how politics helps to form the cultural identity of men and women. This evening I am talking about the overall change that has been nurtured in Europe since the end of the Second World War.

A peaceful globalisation

It is important to recognise that we in the European Union are not alone in searching for a better path. If Europe

21

remains true to its new self, we will form part of an historical trajectory towards 'government for the people' and political communities that respect objective human values and live in peace with one another. Mahatma Gandhi's famous 'talisman' was that in every step he took, he should be accountable to the poorest person in India. Gandhi was the first person to insist that democracy can be made to work by the poor and those who do not enjoy the benefit of literacy and property ownership. Gandhi's legacy is alive, as was evident when the 700 million voters of India changed their government in 2004.

Europe and India are the two largest democratic societies in the world. What has happened in our continent and South Asia has its counterpart at a global level.

In the nineteenth century, in the officers' messes, country houses and gentlemen's clubs of the so-called civilised world, the elites of society held to opinions on women's rights, workers' rights, racial theory and religious exclusivity that today would be seen as bizarre in any student canteen. Governments had great difficulty shaking off the idea that contracts for the ownership of slaves should be honoured in civil law. That is why the United States had its Civil War, the first of the great wars of attrition.

We are fortunate to have acquired in the twentieth century a new perspective on the 'truth about man'. Since the Universal Declaration of Human Rights we know how to insist that 'the Sabbath exists for man, not man for the Sabbath'. No interest of state can override fundamental rights of conscience or fundamental rights to the fulfilment of basic needs. From now on, since the Universal Declaration and the UN Charter, we have the moral confidence to judge all civilisations by a humanistic criterion. As the third millennium begins, we do not need to hold things together by making idols of the names of our individual countries or empires. We are not afraid of truth, beauty and love in the public space.

The first astronauts gave us a physical perspective to correspond to the moral perspective of the Universal Declaration. Taking pictures of our globe 'from a distance', as the song goes, the astronauts offered us a new way of

seeing ourselves. This twentieth-century icon of our float-
ing globe, so tiny in the great spaces of the universe,
prompts us to accept responsibility for our environment. It
prompts us to seek a more unified understanding of
human history. The premise of such a unified history is our
vulnerability. The building blocks of such a history are continents and centuries – even millennia.

The third millennium will test whether mankind is capable, in the interests of our own survival, of a different quality of civilisation. The continent of Europe is the original
motor of globalisation and the source of both the democratic ideal and our modern conception of the rights of
man. In terms of cultural tradition, Europe is the most
Christianised of all the continents. A great deal is at stake
for mankind in the success of the Europe of Reconciliation
for, make no mistake about it, founding treaties about steel
and coal were built on the human gifts of forgiveness, of
transcendence of bitterness, of friendship-building among
the most resentful enemies, of consensus-building out of
the ruins of conflict. Somewhere in the debris of the dismal
first half of twentieth-century Europe, a group of men and
women consciously decided to try love and not hate, to put
into radical action the great commandment to love one
another. Hate had been tried. Its diabolical consequences
were painfully transparent. Through the nightmare, rare
relief had come from individual and collective acts of hero-
ism and courage, decency and unselfishness, generosity
and sacrifice. The founders of the Union believed in the
unrevealed strength of the human spirit, not its manifest
weakness. They believed that we were capable of creating
a better world and they set out to prove it. The success of
our reconciled Europe has converted many with very trou-
bled pasts, Bulgaria and Romania, Croatia and Turkey, to
seek to be part of the vision. Parts of the Balkans still teeter
uncertainly on the brink of conflict. They too face the
choice of peace and prosperity or war and misery.

Elements of risk

I have suggested how fortunate we are that that 'Europe'
was conceived in the aftermath of the two World Wars. I

have suggested that our Europe is not an only child, but has cousins and other relatives in the post-war world. I want now to bring the troubling news. Europe is an infant still – a robust infant, but nevertheless an infant. Therefore, it is in need of care, nourishment and protection if it is to reach proper maturity, if it is both to grow up and to act grown-up.

It is appropriate to look at some of the risks we face, some of the elements of turbulence that make it difficult for the Europe of Reconciliation to live up to its vocation.

Making the long-term case for Europe

The first risk I want to identify – and I know it is a hard saying – is that of a superficial analysis of our economic situation. Have we become too accustomed to the idea of Europe as a provider of purely economic benefits?

I am thinking of questions like these: Do we sufficiently recognise that cohesion and stability within the Union are achieved sometimes at a price, the price of investing in our common programmes? Do we sufficiently understand that consensus and fair trade at the international level are also bought at a price? Are we prepared to recognise that economic buoyancy, as currently measured, is not always guaranteed?

The psychological complication is that membership of the European Union has coincided for most of us with a clear transformation for the better of our economic life. The new member states aspire to similar progress. We need to hold two ideas in mind simultaneously. First, the scale of the European Union makes it the best available platform for economic growth, and growth can enable us to do some very worthwhile things. But, second, economic growth is by no means the sole test of the European Union.

The European Constitution describes the core values of the Union as: 'founded on the values of respect for human dignity, freedom, democracy, equality, the rule of law and respect for human rights, including the rights of persons belonging to minorities...'. Our commitment to a common future and to respecting these values will remain whether in good or less favourable times. It is in no one's interest for expectations of short-term gain to become so entrenched that the long-term common good of Europe and her children plays little part in the debate. That would be to enter into dangerous territory. Is it in anyone's interest to undermine European reconciliation or collapse the mechanisms of European co-operation because of some pressure of the moment or some secondary disagreement? To allow this to happen would certainly not be a sign of growing up.

I am saying, in other words, that our understanding of Europe should rely less on short-term arguments than on the broad-based and long-term 'structural' case – economic, political and cultural – for coming together in the historic voluntary partnership of sovereign states that is European Union.

Respect for difference

Europe is home to many political perspectives, many cultures, many traditions and heritages. We speak many languages. We accommodate religious differences. Most of Europe's member states are secular states, though others, as here in England, have established Churches, but they have all come through the crucible of change, forged by histories in which religious conflict formed a not inconsiderable part. We are a very long way from those revolutionary days in the 1790s when the political-religious structure of the day was succinctly articulated by King George III who said (1798), 'No country can be governed where there is more than one established religion: the others may be tolerated but that cannot extend further than leave to perform their religious duties according to the tenets of their church, for which indulgence they cannot have any share in the government of the state.'

Today throughout Europe every citizen is entitled to share in the government of the state and in full civic life regardless of religious belief, not because of governmental indulgence, but by an acknowledged birthright that is antecedent to and morally superior to any law, any system that would attempt to deny it.

Ancient Roman legions and modern markets are monuments to the standardisation that often goes with power.

25

The Europe of Reconciliation is not naïve about the need to organise. But our vocation as Europeans, both within the Union and in relation to our neighbours, is to acknowledge diversity and arrive at stable, co-operative relationships through working the common ground. We reject the either/or thinking of the zero sum game. Our institutions are complex and balanced. They are square circles. We have rehabilitated the notions of coalition and compromise and, as John Hume would say, we are prepared to shed our sweat together in order to forge trust. We are learning the strength that comes from working together instead of accepting the wastefulness that comes from working against one another or simply ignoring one another.

Too often in the past, political power has been tempted to fall back on the utilitarian principle that the end justifies the means. An important aspect of growing up in Europe is to turn this around and allow the quality of the means we choose to provide the justification of the ends. Every time we react to a provocation with restraint, every time we say of our opponent that, if he is not a hundred per cent right, he may be ten or twenty per cent right, we are creating the space out of which a civilisation of love – that phrase that Cardinal Hume always used – can continue to grow.

I would go so far as to say that respect for difference constitutes the European method. It has taken our continent a long time to learn that, in situations of conflict or mutual contradiction, all of us carry a burden imposed by circumstances and must help one another cast off that burden.

If respect for difference is the European badge, we must be very concerned indeed about the manifestations in our midst of racism and intolerance. Such incidents are the points at which the European fabric can begin to unravel. They bring us back to Europe's original sin. They remind us that the contemptuous classification of peoples was the shibboleth, the monstrous lie, at the root of both the slave trade and the holocaust.

I cannot offer a policy prescription in this area but offer some thoughts. Our educational systems should openly address the challenges of a multi-faceted culture. We should look for both symbolic and practical ways to affirm the solidarity of different groups in our society while encouraging the widest possible, comfortable, social integration, an integration that does not demand the obliteration of identity or culture but which lives easily with multiple tracks running through one human life. We should be reminded of the shared history and values of the great Abrahamic faiths, Judaism, Islam and Christianity and of the great wisdom and principles of the many other world faith systems, each of which opens to us a particular perspective on life, on death and on faith, each of which holds its own unique part of the immense jigsaw puzzle which is humankind's relationship with existence and with God. We should work towards a European consensus on immigration. We should avoid defining the relationship between Christianity and Islam in geopolitical terms. We should recognise in racism one more warning sign regarding what has been called the 'atomisation' of modern society, a subject to which I will return in a moment.

The need for historical reference points

It is a necessary condition of growing up that we learn from our mistakes. 'To be human is to change and to be perfect is to have changed often,' said Cardinal Newman. But change of itself is not enough for we are just as capable of changing for the worse as for the better and the process of growing up insists that we should get better, wiser, less capricious, more resilient. For change to mean 'growing up', we need to see how changes, including setbacks and our responses to setbacks, lead us forward along a path.

The Risen Christ had wounds when he appeared to Thomas. Perhaps it is true too that our culture needs to carry the evidence of our wounds into the future if we are to continue to learn from our mistakes.

In two World Wars, we looked into the abyss. We saw that social organisation and technological skill had reached the point where humankind was capable of destroying not only everything we believe in but even the very world we live in. In the late 1940s, people of vision said 'never again' and began to draw the necessary conclusions. Unfortunately amnesia sets in quickly and there is a very real possibility that we will lose this historical memory, this essential preface to the modern European story. As new glib voices dilute or gloss that memory, it is worth remembering the voices of those who were victims of that historic, endemic culture of unhealthy national rivalries with their ugly assertions of cultural or ethnic or political superiority. As we try to seedbed a new culture of reconciliation and respect, the protective scaffolding around this new, fragile construct is our ever-fresh and humbling memory of those depths to which humanity has so often descended and the historical reference points which teach us about the dark side of power, passion and patriotism.

Solidarity towards other peoples

I turn now to a fourth condition for the safeguarding of the European ideal – we will only discover a true and rooted European identity in openness and solidarity towards other peoples. It is a paradox of our time that political communities which in the past never lacked energy to sustain conflict and war often have difficulty mobilising themselves for engagement with today's global agenda, particularly the agenda of poverty and disease eradication.

The world is getting smaller. Satellite television, the Internet and e-commerce point to the most salient feature of the information and communications revolution, namely the permeability of traditional boundaries. The sheer volume and variety of connections that are now possible represent a qualitative difference as compared to the connections of the past. That is why we tend to say 'integration' when we describe globalisation today. Twenty years ago, or even ten years ago, we might have used the word 'interdependence'.

The main economic significance of the digital revolution is the speed and scale of activity that now becomes possible, and its low cost. This has accelerated long-term trends. The global market was already growing exponentially for a number of reasons, including the welfare state, population growth, the opening of markets since World War Two, the end of the Cold War and the consequent spread of a particular model of economic and social development. From 1950 to 2000, world production increased by a factor of five and the volume of merchandise trade multiplied by a factor of about twenty. Developments in China and India are likely to ensure that this trend continues. At the same time, since 1950, the number of people in the world has more than doubled. Then it was 2.5 billion. Soon it will be 7 billion. We know that the exponential rate of increase will continue for some time more, raising issues of water and fuel scarcity, global warming and migration from poorer countries to richer countries.

These long-term trends are brought about largely by factors over which governments do not always exercise immediate control. However, with so much happening, so much raw force in play, it is not surprising that there are concerns over widening inequality, the emergence of new concentrations of power, and the possible loss of democratic control.

For me, the statistics about preventable deaths and preventable disease among infants and small children in the third world are a sharp reality-check when the praises are chanted of market-driven globalisation. The culture of solidarity which cements the European Union, the twinning of interests, the sharing of prosperity is, and ultimately should always be, a solidarity which embraces the entire human family, in particular in all its most pitiful conditions. A prosperity built on their poverty is no great badge of honour and neither is a prosperity which overlooks their poverty. The forces of globalisation, from which have come and will come so many benefits to us Europeans, must also be subject to a wider accountability in which we acknowledge and help to vindicate the rights of those whose lives are mired in the poverty, disease, corruption and ignorance which characterise the experience of the vast majority of those with whom we share this little planet. Their reliance on our honesty and integrity is even more profound than their reliance on our generosity and our aid. Self-evidently the European Union can play a worthy part in rendering the forces of globalisation more accountable to the peoples of the United Nations and in giving leadership in the politics and practice of effective global solidarity.

29

Addressing the atomisation of society

I come now to a fifth and final angle on safeguarding the Europe of Reconciliation, namely – if I may borrow a phrase – the pursuit of happiness. The measurement of happiness as opposed to freedom of choice is an emerging field in economics. What is the advantage of a higher income if the quality of life experienced day to day is eroded by the pressures and problems that a very busy consumer culture of individual achievement often produces?

For all our new-found individual confidence, enhanced education and opportunity there are plenty of indicators of deep-seated unhappiness and plenty of indicators of stresses within families – enough to challenge our easy assumptions that healthy economic indicators will, without more of something else, bring a smile to every face.

And there are many other indicators of unhappiness in Europe today – the widespread voter apathy and cynicism about politics, the declining birth rate, the suicide rate among the young and the elderly, the abuse of mood-enhancing drugs whether lawful alcohol or unlawful drugs, the random acts of violence, including racist violence, the road rage and football rage, the atomisation of society in which many thousands of children's playtimes with parents depend on interventions by lawyers and courts, the Europe where many of the elderly live lives of quiet loneliness.

You are right if you are thinking many another generation faced worse and each pays a price for its own priorities and yes, we have our good news to tell. We are beginning to open up to the wonder of the abilities of the disabled, to the crying needs of carers, to the wasted talents of early school leavers. Our world is full of second chances, of new, insistent voices telling us their story, setting out their ambitions, driving us on to deal with each other more humanly, more lovingly, more carefully. Yes – you are also right that if the generations had a choice of which generation they would be born into, many of those who have gone before us would join the queue for our generation, for our times, for with all their ups and all their downs these are indeed the best of times for a greater number of people. But all around us are the signs of work to be done, of jobs not yet completed, of men, women and children, who feel like mere spectators at this feast of plenty.

The signs of our times are full of contradictions. How do we respond to them? Do we live only for ourselves and for the moment or do we continue the work of Europe's founding fathers by resolutely articulating and advocating a vision of a world where the meeting point of politics, economics, culture and religion converges in a world of equals who treat each other and their planet with a resounding respect that forms a gift of intelligent, caring stewardship to the generations yet to come?

That friendship is possible between people of vast differences within the EU is wonderfully reassuring but, make no mistake, it doesn't happen by doing nothing – it only happens when one human being decides to bridge the chasm by reaching out a hand, risking rejection but taking the risk in the hope of revealing the smiling 'yesness' that has always been there in the heart of the estranged other.

We are blessed to grow up in today's Europe and to watch the discipline of friendship reveal to us, Europe's children, for the very first time our true potential, our yesness to each other and our power for good when we work respectfully together. As someone once so wisely said: the best is yet to come.

3 Christianity in Europe

Timothy Radcliffe OP

The contribution of Christianity to the future of Europe

Just over a week ago, the new Pope chose the name 'Benedict'. Benedict is co-patron of Europe, along with Francis of Assisi and the Dominican Catherine of Siena. At his first general audience he explained that he chose this name because of his concern for the future of Christianity in Europe, which is just the topic I have been asked to address this evening.

When I was last in Brussels, one of my brethren gave me two books by Eric-Emmanuel Schmitt, *Monsieur Ibrahim et les fleurs du Coran* and *Oscar et la dame rose*. These books are a publishing sensation! *Oscar* sold over 400,000 copies in the first year; they have been on the best-selling lists in France, Belgium, Germany and Italy. I read them in the plane on the way home. I must confess that when I finished *Oscar* I was literally moved to tears. The stewardess came to see whether I was all right, and I persuaded her to console me with another little bottle of wine! These books tell one much about what people hope for from religion in Europe today.

In each of these books you see a child who is facing death. Momo, a young Jew, must witness the death of his beloved Sufi teacher, Ibrahim; Oscar is a child without any religion who faces death with the help of an ancient Christian female wrestler, Mamie Rose. These children know little about religion, but they are looking for God. In both books, religion is linked to personal experience rather than doctrine. In Ibrahim's Qur'an there are two dried flowers and a letter from his friend. These are his inspiration rather than Islamic doctrine. In an interview Schmitt said that his task was to pose questions rather than to give answers. He said, 'Les questions rassemblent alors que les réponses divisent' ('Questions gather people together while answers divide'). That gives one a snap-shot of the Europe that the new Pope wishes to evange-lise. It is not secularised. There is a deep hunger for God. People do not look to Christianity alone but to all the great religions. The young especially are interested in spirituality rather than doctrine. They are interested in God more than the Church. They are greatly preoccupied by death

The European Values Studies (EVS), which are con-ducted every ten years, confirm all this. The 1999 survey showed an increase in the number of people who described themselves as religious and in belief in the afterlife, espe-cially among the young. But attendance at religious cere-monies is continuing to drop. So Europe has been described as 'believing without belonging'. Schmitt's nov-els hit the bull's eye.

Clearly a big challenge for Christianity is how to remain in contact with the millions of people who look for God but do not come to church. At the centre of Christianity is com-munity; we are gathered by the Lord around the altar. How can we attract people to belong as well as believe? How can we put bums on pews? Thanks be to God, I do not have to answer that question since the Cardinal will when he talks about the future shape of the Church next month. Good luck, Cardinal Cormac! Instead I have been asked to explore another question: What contribution may Christianity make to the future of Europe?

Schmitt wrote a trilogy of books. The heroes are Chris-tian, Jewish, Muslim and Buddhist. The old Christendom has gone. The Europe that we are called by Pope Benedict to evangelise is the home of all the faiths of the world. The key question for the future of Europe is whether these faiths will live together in peace or whether they will tear Europe apart.

Sam Harris wrote in *The Times* last month:

> One of the greatest challenges facing civilization in the 21st cen-tury is for human beings to speak about their deepest concerns – about ethics, spiritual experience, and human suffering – in ways that are not flagrantly irrational. Incompatible religious doctrines have Balkanised our world and these divisions have

become a continuous source of bloodshed... Words like 'God' and 'Allah' must go the way of 'Apollo' and 'Baal' or they will unmake our world.

And one can understand his position. All over the world people are fighting each other in the name of religion. Once again in Europe there is growing anti-Semitism, and tensions between Christians and Muslims are escalating, especially in tolerant Holland.

Christianity will only make a contribution to the future of Europe if it can prove that people like Sam Harris are wrong and that we can make peace. Another reason that the Pope chose the name Benedict was in honour of Benedict XV, a man who sought peace during the First World War. When asked if he was neutral during the war, he replied, 'Neutral, not impartial!'

Christians can bring peace to multi-religious Europe because we are able to understand the role of faith in the lives of other believers better than atheists. In 1989, France was split by the *affaire du foulard*, the controversy over Muslim girls wearing headscarves to school. It was Christian leaders who understood why it mattered to them, people like the Archbishop of Marseille and the Archbishop of Canterbury. We Christians could identify with the Muslims. After all, if they could not wear their foulards, then why should nuns be allowed to wear their veils in school? I believe that it is still technically illegal for religious orders to wear their habits in public in England and so I am at this moment liable to be arrested! So if you feel that this lecture goes on too long, then just ring for the police!

In 1974 the French Catholic Church established the Secrétariat pour les Relations avec l'Islam. Visit the website! You will discover Christians being invited to share Ramadan with Muslims, and Muslims to share Lent with us. There is advice on how to raise children of Muslim/ Christian marriages. Young Muslims from St Ouen charmingly wished French Christians a happy Christmas with an Irish blessing. In Britain, CAFOD works closely with Islamic Relief. So the first contribution that Christianity must make to the future of Europe is to help other believers to feel at home. Religion may tear Europe apart or knit it together. Christianity first made Europe into Christendom. Now our challenge is to help Europe flourish as the home of many faiths. But what about the specific contribution of the gospel? How is the gospel good news for Europe today? Let us go back to Schmitt's two small heroes, Momo and Oscar. They are both pilgrims. Oscar makes a spiritual pilgrimage during the last week of his life, as he lies on his bed quizzing God and his guru, the Christian female wrestler. The Jewish Momo makes a real pilgrimage back to the homeland of his Sufi master. They are both seekers. According to Grace Davie, this is one of the primary ways in which modern Europeans think of their religious identities. Princess Diana typified the modern seeker, getting a little bit of spirituality here and there, a touch of Christianity, a sprinkle of Buddhism, a tasty bit of Sufism. Maybe that is why she is supposed to have got on so well with Cardinal Hume, whose best-known book was *To Be a Pilgrim*.

Pilgrim paths criss-crossed medieval Europe, going to Rome, Jerusalem, Chartres, Santiago de Compostela, Canterbury and hundreds of other places. One might say that Europe was knit together by the paths of pilgrimages. This articulated a profoundly Christian sense that our lives are journeys towards God. The two great classics of Christian spirituality, the *Summa Theologica* of Thomas Aquinas and the *Divina Commedia* of Dante, both see the life of faith as a journey towards happiness.

Today pilgrimages are still flourishing. Five million people go each year to Lourdes, two million to Fatima. Hundreds of thousands walk to Santiago, to hug the statue of St James, dressed like a pilgrim himself. People make their way to Iona, Taizé, Medjugorje and Czêstochowa. Often these pilgrims do not go to church regularly. They do not 'belong' officially. And yet these pilgrimages express some sense that there is something to be sought. As I was waiting to check in at Stansted airport the other day, I saw a sign over the Ryanair desks advertising a book on Science and Medicine. It said, 'Fuel for your spiritual journey.' That's what much of religion is about in Europe today, cheap travel and a spiritual journey. Sometimes it is hard to distinguish pilgrimage from tourism.

It is often said that the end of the twentieth century saw the collapse of the grand master narratives. Fascism, Communism and even, to some extent, Capitalism gave human beings the road maps to paradise, and crucified millions on the way. In July I visited Auschwitz for the first time. At the entrance there is a big map that shows the railway lines from all over Europe leading to the extermination camp. The lines end at the gas chambers. That is literally the end of the line. Rabbi Hugo Gryn describes how, when he arrived at Auschwitz, the entrance to the camp was littered with thrown-away condoms and tefillin. I am not sure what to make of the condoms, but the tefillin were used in Jewish prayer. It was a sign that, here in the camp, there was no point in praying any longer. And Auschwitz has become a place of pilgrimage itself, to remind us what happens when we impose road maps on human beings.

So people are suspicious of anyone who claims to know the road map to paradise. Often it leads to the Killing Fields. But the hunger for a journey still remains. Maybe this is why *The Lord of the Rings* is one of the most popular books ever written. We can identify with Frodo and Sam, setting off not knowing quite where they are going and what they are to do. And Christianity does not offer a road map. We have no more idea than anyone else what will happen in a hundred or a thousand years. But it invites us to set out on the journey and offers a glimpse of the goal.

This evening I wish to suggest that we Christians should accompany people on their pilgrimages. Specifically we should travel with people as they search for the good, the true and the beautiful. According to traditional Catholic theology, human beings are made for these. Every human being hungers for the good, the true and the beautiful. These are desires that are part of our hard wiring. Our contribution is to remind people of these deepest desires, which are rooted in our nature like the migratory urges of salmon or terns, making us restless until we arrive. We should be with people as they search for the good, the beautiful and the true.

To be frank, I suspect that today there is little respect for Christianity as a source of moral teaching about goodness. Most Europeans respect Jesus as a teacher, but not the Churches. This is no doubt partly because priests and the religious have been found guilty of sexual abuse and have lost respect. But the roots are much deeper. It is because the Church's moral teaching usually is thought of as telling people what they must or must not do. The EVS identifies 'individualism' as perhaps the key characteristic of the modern European. This puts a stress on the supreme value of the individual's personal autonomy, on our right to take our own decisions about our lives. We cherish the freedom to decide our moral values. This implies the rejection of excessive interference by any institutions, whether the Church or the State. According to the EVS, the young do look to the Church for spiritual guidance, but overwhelmingly deny any Church any right to personal interference in people's private lives. A religion which conflicts with personal autonomy will be rejected by most modern Europeans.

Also, at the heart of the Church's moral teaching is a vision of the family, of husband and wife living in lifelong mutual fidelity, and having sex so as to produce lots of children. This is indeed a wonderful ideal, and much to be cherished, but most people do not live like that. For better or worse, vast numbers of people are either divorced and remarried, or living with partners, or practising contraception or are in gay relationships. So they will either feel excluded from the Church, or else, if they do wish to belong, then they may either be nagged by guilt or else must mentally shut out this part of the Church's teaching.

What can the Church do? If she stands by her moral teaching, then she will be seen as standing in judgement over a vast percentage of Europeans. One often hears the complaint, 'In the eyes of the Church, I am just a second-class citizen.' If she does not, then she will be seen as surrendering to modernity. If we believe in our moral teaching, then of course we must teach it. Often we try to find a middle way, proclaiming the teaching but quietly letting it be known that it's OK to come to communion. This is called 'the pastoral solution' but it can simply look like dishonesty. I must tell you, before you get too excited, that I do not know the answer. But part of the answer must be to reflect upon what it means for the Church to teach the way to goodness. Seeking the good is not primarily about rules and commandments. It is not about what one is obliged or forbidden to do. Thinking that morality is all about commandments is a relatively new way of thinking, since the Reformation. We need to return to an older vision of theologians like Thomas Aquinas who, as a good Dominican, I must mention from time to time. He saw morality as being primarily about making a journey towards God and happiness. What was central was not the commandments but the virtues. The virtues help one to be a pilgrim.

Virtus means literally 'strength'. The cardinal virtues – courage, prudence, temperance and justice – form one to be strong for the journey. Faith, hope and charity are virtues that give us a glimpse of the end of the journey, life with God. Becoming good is not about submission to rules but about becoming a moral agent, who knows how to struggle with hard decisions and decide which paths to take. Above all the virtues form us for happiness with God. Fergus Kerr OP wrote, 'Thomas Aquinas offers a moral theology, a Christian ethics, centred on one's becoming the kind of person who would be fulfilled only in the promised bliss of face-to-face vision of God.'

If one thinks that being good is fundamentally about obeying rules, then one will focus on individual acts. No sex outside marriage and one must go to Mass every Sunday. And if you fail, then nip into the confessional box and start again. Virtue ethics look at the shape and unity of the whole of human life, as we make our way to God and happiness.

So, one contribution of Christianity to Europe should be to help people in their moral pilgrimage. We must accompany them beginning where they are, regardless of whether this conforms to church teaching. We must not be like the person famously asked the way to Dublin and who replied, 'If I wanted to go to Dublin I would not start here'. We start where people are, even if it is not where the Church says that they ought to be. Samuel Beckett wrote: 'To find form that accommodates the mess, that is the task of the artist.' That is also the task of a pastor. When the good Dominican St Antoninus, Archbishop of Florence, asked Cosimo de Medici to ban all priests from gambling, Cosimo replied wisely, 'First things first. Shouldn't we begin by banning them from using loaded dice?'

Of course there are rules, but they only exist to remind us of the buried desires of our heart. As Herbert McCabe OP wrote, 'Ethics is entirely concerned with doing what you want, that is to say with being free.' Most of the difficulties arise because we do not recognise what we want. And this is exactly the challenge that faces Europeans today. We live in the Free World and do not know how to be happy in our freedom. At the end of the 1990 EVS, Bart McGetrick writes that Europeans need a 'pedagogy of freedom'. Freedom is understood in very limited terms, as the freedom to choose between alternatives, the freedom of the market place. Pepsi Cola or Coca Cola? But this freedom is usually experienced as vacuous. Zygmunt Bauman is a typical modern European, teaching at the Universities of Leeds and Warsaw. He wrote,

> There is a nasty fly of impotence in the tasty ointment of freedom, cooked in the caldron of individualization; that impotence is felt to be all the more odious, discomforting and upsetting in view of the empowerment that freedom was expected to deliver. We are like children who long for a bicycle but then do not know how to ride it.

People should look at Christians and ask themselves, 'What is the secret of their astonishing freedom?' But they do not. To make that contribution to the future of Europe we Christians must ourselves be liberated. St Paul wrote that, 'for freedom Christ has set us free' (Galatians 5:1). If you look at Christians, that is not always obvious. Nietzsche once wrote of Christ that, 'His disciples should look more redeemed.' So we must work to make the Church more obviously a place in which we enjoy the freedom of the children of God.

The next challenge for Christianity is to remind Europeans that we are called to seek the truth. Our society doubts the possibility of arriving at truth and seldom follows the advice of Mark Twain: 'When in doubt, tell the truth. It will confound your enemies and astound your friends.'

The moment that religious leaders start to talk about truth, then people become nervous. And this is understandable. All over the world violence is associated with different faiths quarrelling about the truth. Christians make claims for Jesus, Muslims for the Qu'ran, Hindus for Krishna. These cannot all be true, and so believers start killing each other. Truth claims are associated with intolerance, with arrogance and indoctrination.

This is undeniable. But if the truth cannot be sought, then we shall all just be stuck in our differences. After the Second World War, Albert Camus said in a lecture to the Dominican brethren in Paris, 'Dialogue is only possible between people who remain what they are, and who speak the truth.' There is no point in dialogue if there is no truth. The only basis upon which I may build communion with the believers of other faiths and none is in the shared search for truth. I once caught a taxi, and the taxi driver made some rather racist remarks. I told him that what he was saying was untrue. He replied: 'What do you mean, untrue? They are my opinions.'

Our society has lost confidence in the power of reason, except perhaps scientific reason. Modern Europeans do not trust that through reflection and argument we can discover what is the meaning of human existence, and what is the purpose of our lives. There is little debate around the big questions: Why is there anything rather than nothing? For what am I made? In what may I find my happiness? When people have different convictions, then we tend either to live in mutual tolerance or else beat each other up. Why disagree with someone who thinks that God is a green rabbit, as long as they are happy with the idea?

But we can only draw close to people who think differently if we believe that we can reason together and so learn. Claiming that you have got the truth wrapped up does breed violence and intolerance. Believing that

40

together we may arrive at the truth can heal difference. This is not a fashionable belief. The new Chief Executive of British Airways, Willie Walsh, claimed that 'a reasonable man gets nowhere in negotiations'. Negotiations in our society are not about thinking one's way through to what is best, but trying out one's strength. What matters is winning, and the last resort is the law. Even Parliament does not appear to be a place of much debate.

Paradoxically, one of Christianity's contributions to Europe at this moment should be to believe in reason. Despite all the lunacy of the last century, all the absurdity of war and genocide, we believe that human beings are rational and are made to seek the truth. Hard thinking may heal divisions and further us on the journey. A society which loses confidence in the very possibility of truth ultimately disintegrates. St Augustine called humanity 'the community of truth'. It is the only basis upon which we may belong to each other.

The motto of the Dominican Order is 'Veritas', Truth. I hope that Robert Kilroy-Silk notes that we have had that motto for almost eight hundred years! It is said that Dominic was inspired to found the Order after a night spent in argument with an heretical pub keeper. They debated all night long and, as one of my brethren remarked, Dominic cannot have spent all the time saying, 'You are wrong, you are wrong, you are wrong.' One only goes on arguing because the other person is also in some sense right. We argue not to win but so that the truth can win.

It must infuriate many people that John Paul II saw Christianity as the great defender of reason. In that wonderful Encyclical *Fides et Ratio* he wrote, 'The Church serves humanity with the *diakonia* – the service – of truth.' We are partners in humanity's shared struggle to arrive at truth.

> We see among the men and women of our time, and not just in some philosophers, attitudes of widespread distrust of the human being's great capacity for knowledge. With a false modesty, people rest content with partial and provisional truths, no longer seeking to ask radical questions about the meaning and ultimate foundation of human, personal and social existence.

In a debate between Bertrand Russell and Freddie Copplestone SJ, the question came up as to why the universe existed. Why is there anything rather than nothing? Russell asserted that this is a question that cannot be posed. The universe is just there. It was the Christian philosopher who insisted that he was giving up thinking too soon. So part of our mission in Europe as Christians is to be the people who go on thinking, posing the difficult question, searching for answers.

For the children of the Enlightenment it must seem crazy that the papacy stands up for reason. And yet sociologists have demonstrated from studies in Sweden, Canada and the United States that once people drift away from mainstream Christianity, then they tend to start believing crazy things. According to Rodney Stark, Christians are much less accepting of 'UFOs as alien visitors, of ESP, astrology, Tarot cards, séances, and Transcendental Meditation than students who said they had no religion'. As G.K. Chesterton said, 'A man who won't believe in God will believe in anything.'

So Christianity should remind Europeans of our buried desire for the truth, and walk with them as we search. But we will only be able to do this convincingly if we are seen to be pilgrims ourselves, who do not know all the answers in advance. We must be seen as those who not only teach but also learn. The Church must have the courage to proclaim its convictions, but the humility to learn from other people. Christian leaders will speak with more authority if sometimes they say, 'I do not know'. As Augustine said, 'Whoever thinks that in this mortal life one may so disperse the mists of the imagination as to possess the unclouded light of unchangeable truth... understands neither what he seeks nor who he is that seeks it.'

Let us return for a last time to our two young heroes, Momo and Oscar. They both face death. Momo must witness the death of his Sufi teacher; Oscar faces his own death, with the help of the beloved female wrestler, Mamie Rose. Death is a growing preoccupation of our European contemporaries, and we still turn to the Churches to help us face it. There is a decrease in the number of Christian baptisms and marriages, but people still look to their

Churches to bury them. In France, a relatively secularised country, 70 per cent of the population wish to be buried by the Church. Even President Mitterrand, that well-known agnostic, left an enigmatic instruction before his death, 'une messe est possible'. A Mass is possible. And he had two!

The European Values Study show that a growing percentage of young people believe that there is something after death. For some reason Protestants tend to believe in life after death, but Catholics believe in Heaven. Why is there this concern with death and what follows? Maybe it is the collapse of the grand narratives that dominated the twentieth century. We have lost confidence in any story that can be told about the future of humanity, and so we are more concerned with our own individual story. Does my life lead anywhere? The religion of modern Europe is a pilgrim faith, but does the journey have a final goal, or are we going nowhere?

As Christians we share our hope, for each person and for humanity. We really are on our way to happiness. And one way that we express that hope is through beauty. C.S. Lewis said that beauty rouses up the desire for 'our own far-off country', the home for which we long and have never seen.

Modern Europeans are resistant to church teaching. Dogma is a bad word! But beauty has its own authority, an authority to which every human being responds, and an authority that in no way threatens. We need to find ways of disclosing God's beauty to our contemporaries. We must give people a glimpse of Christ's beauty, for as Augustine said:

> He is beautiful in Heaven, beautiful on earth:
> beautiful in the womb, beautiful in his parents' hands:
> beautiful in his miracles; beautiful under the scourge:
> beautiful when inviting to life; beautiful also when not
> regarding death; beautiful in laying down his life;
> beautiful in taking it up again; beautiful on the cross;
> beautiful in the Sepulchre; beautiful in heaven.

It is said that once in the sixties George Patrick Dwyer, that terrifying and irascible Archbishop of Birmingham, went

43

to attend a parish Mass. The parish had prepared a rich liturgy, with the most modern songs accompanied by lots of guitars. And halfway through one song, the Archbishop slammed the hymn-book shut and shouted, 'Enough of these trivial ditties. Let's sing something decent. Turn to page 82 [or whatever].' At the end of the Mass, the parish priest thanked everyone for their contribution and then publicly apologised for the dreadful rudeness of the Archbishop. There was an awful silence and then Archbishop Dwyer said, 'Well, I have something to say. At least there is one courageous priest in this diocese.'

But one has a certain sympathy with the Archbishop's irritation. I hope that I never again have to break bread together on my knees! We need to find an aesthetic that does speak of God's beauty. Beauty is not an added extra, icing on the liturgical cake. It is of the essence. Every great revival of Christianity has gone with some new exploration of beauty, from the Post-Tridentine Baroque, which I do not like much, to Wesley's hymns. Surely this Cathedral is an attempt to give us a glimpse of paradise, sustaining us in the belief that the journey is going somewhere, and that one day we shall arrive.

Recently I was in the Philippines for a meeting of Asian Dominicans. One night our Pakistani brothers and sisters played a video of a Sufi singer. He was a rather unattractive, fat, androgynous figure, but when he began to sing we were enchanted. A sister gave me a rough translation of his words, but it was evident that he was struggling with the boundaries of what could be said. The music was reaching for the unsayable. How often do our liturgies pull apart the veil even for a moment?

In the words of St Ephrem the Syrian:

> The Lord of all is the treasure store of all things:
> Upon each according to his capacity He bestows a glimpse
> Of the beauty of His hiddenness, of the splendour of His majesty...
> All who look upon You will be sustained by Your beauty.
> Praises be to Your splendour.

So, to conclude, Christianity must accompany our European pilgrims as they journey, seeking the good, the true and the beautiful. It is not enough just to talk about them. Otherwise our words will be empty. We must work hard to make the Church evidently a place of abundant freedom, with a passion for truthfulness and a delight in beauty.

4 Europe in Solidarity

Bob Geldof

(The following was the basis for the talk given by Bob Geldof)

'Be yourself. Rediscover your origins. Relive your roots'. That is the order that Pope John Paul II gave in his exhortation to Europe, *Ecclesia in Europa*.

But if we Europeans are not Irish, English, Polish, then who are we? What does being European mean? What *are* our roots? The Pope urged us to rediscover our true identity around 'a new model of unity in diversity, as a community of reconciled nations open to the other continents and engaged in the present process of globalisation'. Well, on current projections for the above-mentioned ambition, 'Pigs will fly'.

But my starting point must be that an almost impossible tension is emerging between that European ideal and the reality. As Europe grows it is becoming unable to show solidarity towards itself, let alone its partners or, worse, the poorest people of the world. Unless we pause and examine ourselves, Europe is in danger of constructing itself into being nothing more than an exclusive rich man's club, an autistic union of comfort that does not feel responsible to its neighbours or the poor of the world.

In this talk tonight, I want to argue that Europe will never mean anything unless it looks beyond itself, to live up to what it claims as common European values. We have had centuries of colonialism and war followed by decades of introversion. But we will not be able to find ourselves, or relive our roots unless we come, like all great cultures, to a common sense of our responsibility to the rest of the world: a solidarity that is ultimately in our common interest.

Solidarity in Europe was never part of the original prospectus. Although it is mentioned as one of the principles in the Schuman Declaration which founded the

European Community in 1950, Europe has never had a motivating vision like the American dream. But the American dream was built upon an extraordinary collective act of willed amnesia whereby Americans were allowed to believe that they could forget their miserable past on this great new continental *tabula rasa*. Europe cannot shuck off its past so easily. There is no *terra nova* for this old continent. To use the Americanism, we carry our baggage with us like overburdened turtles – slowly, ponderously, heavily weighing our psychologies so that no bureaucratic structure or papal edict can remove the awful scars of memory. Perhaps a solidarity of trauma. But that is thin ground upon which to build the new model Europe. Instead, Europe has drawn all of its energy from failure. Unlike America the European Project can be seen in many ways as an escape route from historical trauma, political failure, philosophical depravity, war, genocide and economic backwardness.

The great sum of European thought must be the idea of the individual. It is hard to see the shibboleth of 'I' emerging from another continent. From the Judaeo-Christian notion, the sacred Western ideal of the sanctity of individual life, through the God-like Ego Sum, what other continent could give us the Magna Carta, habeas corpus, the Reformation, the Enlightenment, 'I think, therefore I am'? Descartes had to be European. Where else but Europe would the identification of the primary psychological motor of the individual in society be defined as the ego or the revolutionary idea of human rights whereby each individual is made inviolate through inalienable entitlements?

If there are many European cultures framed around the pan-continental 'I', then it makes it more difficult to have a solidarity of 'Us'. An identifiable 'We'. In order to find solidarity we need to find first who we are. And it will not be found in the dead air of the Eurocrat's office nor mandated by bureaucrats' fiat flags or mawkish ersatz anthems.

Europe's child America was founded primarily on the individual's need for essentially unfettered existence: the need for 'I' to pursue its individual happiness. And still, through its constant myth-making movies, America perpetuates the ultimate individual pitted against unknowable, conspiratorial bodies who wish somehow to hem or curtail that independence. We somehow are beginning to feel something of that in our Union and it is making us uneasy. The individual is always exceptional, entire unto himself, only responsible for his own actions. Take this to its conclusion and you arrive at the modern state which practises a dangerous form of national exceptionalism, answerable to no one but themselves and pursuing their own agenda regardless of another.

In Europe, on the other hand, we've had our fair share of charismatic leaders who have consistently led us to disaster or saved us as we gazed mesmerised by the individual brilliance or the mad charisma and slavishly followed the superior one. Of course the irony and paradox of individualism is that it can only ever work when it acts in concert for the common good. *'E pluribus unum'*: an occasional solidarity of purpose but not the same as hero-worship; a dull worthy glow of community versus the crazed mercury high of the Golden One; the lunatic savant.

Europe has had its fair share of charismatic leaders like Churchill and Napoleon and sundry unmentionables. But the people who built the EU were almost anonymous technocrats who were trying to escape from the interminable grand plans and charisma that had brought the continent to its knees. When French poet Paul Valéry said, 'we hope vaguely, we dread precisely', he could not know that is exactly what has happened as each country has joined the European Union for its own reasons. We know our past, we know each other, and we fear ourselves. We seek protection from unwieldy neighbours, or a route back to international respectability, or a market for our countries' goods. As Mark Leonard shows in his wildly optimistic new book, *Why Europe Will Run the 21st Century*, Europe is a continent with a past it wants to escape rather than a future it wants to build together.

Unless you understand how you got to where you are, moving on can only be a fearful shuffling forward into a blind man's bluff future. Idealistic Eurocrats have pretended the past is of no consequence to the European project. We start anew. Year Zero is Maastricht. But it's not, and all of us know this because we live who we are. We live the past by the hour.

It is the great conceit of the Eurocrat that history has been disappeared by bureaucratic sleight of hand but it is also the great unspoken truth of the European citizenry that it has not. And it is precisely that murderous history which is driving us reluctantly, suspiciously together.

European integration started with coal and steel production, tariffs and customs unions – rather than a 'European dream' set out by politicians. The unfortunate, unromantic result is that the Union we live in today is not only a paper tiger but literally a paper mountain, to go presumably alongside the other wasted mountains of unwanted butter and wheat. Europe has been built upon 80,000 pages of legislation that regulate everything from the composition of tomato paste to the protection of minorities, generating an irritated resentment at what is perceived as unwarranted, unwelcome interference in the personal by an anonymous chimera, as opposed to what is meant to be achieved, which if one listens to the overblown and hubristic propaganda, is a glad and grateful overpowering sense of belonging.

The European Union has at times introduced flags, and anthems, and passports to try and make us feel European, but most of the time European integration has taken a back seat to national identity. Its laws are passed by national parliamentarians, policed by national law courts, and implemented by national ministers. And that is the way we like it. For excellent historic reasons there is little appetite today for our governments to hand over control over cherished policies like tax, health, education, defence and pensions to a European superstate in Brussels. And to be fair to the founders of the European Union, they have never tried to build a country called Europe.

But as a result of this essentially bureaucratic construct, Europe does feel slightly empty, even suburban as an ideal – almost like what the planners of Milton Keynes would have come up with. A continent of Pooterish ambition. Even if you wanted it to, Europe cannot lift its eyes or soar – it is an almost secret project. Not disguised as such but more hidden in plain sight behind a deluge of seemingly impertinent, alarmingly intrusive, and always incomprehensible edicts. It is and will remain a techno-cratic project of bureaucrats, sealed in the hundreds of thousands of meetings that take place between national officials every year, rather than a political project that takes centre-stage in election campaigns, that brings demonstrators to the streets, that inspires new political parties or movements.

The paradox is that this very same invisibility that led to the best of the European Union's successes in the past may be the thing that destroys it in the future. Because in the beginning Europe did not impinge too much on our daily lives, we were willing to go along with it. And even its harshest critics would agree that for good or ill, and I believe largely for good, it has silently changed our coun-tries beyond recognition: fifty years of common Soviet threat formed common purpose and a common economic integration which has brought peace, prosperity and very high levels of economic cohesion to a set of countries exhausted by a succession of wars. And the bureaucratic unification of our states has been paralleled by a remark-able convergence in the attitudes and lifestyles of Europeans. As wealth grew, the rise of consumerism, secu-larism, falling birth rates, and shifts to more liberal social agendas have marched in ragged step across Europe. The cheap-fare Easyjet generation find it as convenient to hop across to Dublin or Madrid as to go to Blackpool or Bournemouth. And with money, ease of transport and free trade we are all eating more or less the same food: the shelves in Sainsbury's and Tesco groan under the weight of Danish bacon, Irish butter, Greek olives, Italian pasta, French cheese, Belgian beer and English pork pies.

But because this process of unification went on behind closed doors, European citizens do not give even a reluc-tant credit to it for any of the successes of the last fifty years. Instead they focus overmuch on the failures. Some see not welcome unification but a sad homogenisation of living; the bureaucrats' beloved standardisation; an ironing out of difference and diversity; a great flattening of life. They rightly complain about excessive regulation, fraud and a distant bureaucracy in Brussels. Indeed the mental image of the Brussels' Eurocrat has been already painted by another famous Belgian: Magritte's little faceless man in the bowler hat and brolly staring off into nothing. And there is, let's face, it a great deal of the surreal about the whole Euro project. A willingness to accept as reality that which only exists in the fevered mind of the Euro managers.

Although many Europeans may feel a common sense of fate they do not see how EU institutions respond to it. For ten years large majorities understanding the globalised nature of such concerns have favoured common European rather than national action to deal with environmental problems, poverty, international crime, and even foreign and defence policy. However, this has not translated either into any affection for institutions in Brussels, itself a child of the globalised world or much of a sense of solidarity with other countries across Europe.

European countries live in self-interested amity rather than in common proprietorial solidarity. One can clearly see how my native Ireland has gained from European benefits – there is hardly a single road, rail or other infrastructural change that doesn't have a sign acknowledging the EU for its financial support. And Greece, Spain and Portugal have all benefited from major fiscal transfers from richer countries. But as the EU has enlarged, its cohesion but not its rationale has been stretched to its limits. In many ways the year 2003 was a turning point. Our poor uncherished European Community shattered into a thousand factions: old versus new; big versus small; south versus east; social integrationists versus liberal expansionists. The bottom line is that German office workers do not want to subsidise Polish peasants, French factory workers are scared of competition from Slovaks, and everyone seems uneasy with Turkey. We cannot speak with a single voice on the world stage, and we cannot agree where our borders should lie.

In the 1990s, European leaders focused disgracefully on passing the Maastricht Treaty while the Balkans burned. Europeans put their internal economic and bureaucratic cohesion above their responsibilities to their neighbours. But you cannot erect a new iron curtain, or perhaps for

Europe a brocade curtain, to shut yourselves off from global problems. As hundreds of thousands of Bosnians came to our borders we turned, as ever despite the rhetoric, to Washington and prayed for help. A few years later in Kosovo, European governments were belatedly part of the solution as well as the problem. And finally in Macedonia they acted before a crisis turned into a tragedy.

When I sang with my old band, The Boomtown Rats, I played all over Europe, from Brussels to Barcelona to Bucharest, Vigo to Vilnius, from Genoa to the Gdansk ship yards. Thirty years of travel showed me the deep bond of intellectual identity that holds Eastern and Western Europe together. There is such a thing as a European culture and it co-exists alongside European cultures. Brussels seems to misunderstand this. They call it a European ideal. There isn't one of those but there is a European idealism and it is this that has been perverted into a wholly unconvincing Euro polity. And although we finally stumbled our way into taking responsibility for our neighbourhood at the beginning of the twenty-first century – begrudgingly enlarging to let in the former Soviet States – European citizens, perhaps in retreat from the moral disaster of colonialism, still lack an ethic of global responsibility. Euro romantics feel that enlargement to the East was a tryst with destiny for our continent rather than an economic and defence imperative. But this historic process of enlargement did not spring forth from deep reserves of solidarity. Ultimately it was a bureaucratic process that barely impinged on its citizens' consciousness and, when it did, it was with a deep unease and misgivings activating dormant atavistic fears of the Eastern hordes. The main debates were, politically and correctly, dealing with the problems of migration, farming subsidies and voting weights in the European Council – rather than the idealistic opportunity for a Europe that is whole and free and together.

As political Europe becomes bigger, lines of countries are forming to share in our success. The revolutions in Georgia and Ukraine were a plea to share in our wealth and freedoms. The Turks are also banging on our door and here those fears become tangible and sometimes unfairly unhinged. Still, can the Turks accept our freedoms and the cultural and philosophical foundations that come with them as they surely do incredibly and uniquely in America? But it is our inability to set out a common project that can bind people together within our continent that is stopping us from engaging with each other or our neighbours. It is creating a suffocatingly smug wall of satisfaction that hermetically seals us off from our responsibilities to the world.

I don't want to knock the European project – because we are better off with it than without it – but we do need to find a way of closing the gaping gap that has opened up between its unresponsive, free-floating political class, this ENA-ocracy that has driven European integration and Europe's citizens. It is now fifteen years since Jacques Delors said, 'Europe began as an elitist project where all that was necessary was to convince decision-makers. That phase of benign despotism is over.' But it isn't. The symptoms still persist. There is profound unease about the European Union that becomes apparent every time the European project meets the public: in Denmark, in Ireland, and even in the bastions of old Europe – or the polls in France today. At best there is a resigned reluctance and an unengaged reticence to being hauled like braying donkeys into something we don't trust and is inexplicably unanswerable and unknowable to us: a brave new Eurofuture.

I would like Europe to work but we need to understand why there is no solidarity, rather than pretending that everything is fine. We need to stop and think, where do we go from here? We need to build on the Western idea of the individual. We have extended that to the East, but now that we have got there we need to find things to bind us together – in the absence of a Soviet threat. The simple truth is that we don't have the same common feeling for people in Bulgaria that people in the United States under the cult of the flag or the fetish of the constitution feel for someone from Minneapolis or Texas. And we will not get it by taking refuge in our Christian past, or seeing ourselves ridiculously as a counterweight to American power, at a time when China's and India's success is the big story of our time. I suggest this must be the real challenge.

But no matter how frustrating the tension between ideal and reality becomes, the solution cannot be to retreat behind our protectionist fences, our very large, well-tended hedge; to retreat fearfully behind the fusty embrace of our brocade curtain. Europe cannot exist by or unto itself any more than the UK can. It must engage with the world. Beyond duty, it is a necessity.

Let's look at it in a way with which I am familiar: the relationship of Europe with Africa. A very simple way of looking at it is this: were the UK alone to donate its entire GDP to Africa it still would not relieve the poverty or resolve the misery of those African people and it would simply compound ours. Britain like almost everywhere, including America, can no longer function in isolation. And neither can Europe and certainly not Africa.

The North coast of Africa is just eight miles from Europe, but it could be in another world. Africa has slipped out of the world safety net. It drifts away from us propelled by the enormity of their poverty and our exhausted indifference. Twenty years ago next year I stood in the death camps of northern Ethiopia. As far as I could see in the denuded and blasted moonscape about me, people, often naked, streamed out of the hills and plains in long lines to a place they'd heard others had come to sit and wait and die perhaps, until someone found them and could maybe help. The anger I felt then has lasted twenty years.

But on a visit to Ethiopia last year I felt a different, newer despair. This time everything was green, but the people were still starving. They were used to the irregular rainfalls, and would normally allow for the subsequent crop failures and food shortages by profitably selling their coffee on the world market and buy in whatever food they needed to make up that year's shortfall. Except this year the price of coffee had collapsed by 70 per cent because Vietnam, a country they had never heard of, had entered the market a continent away and depressed the world market price. We call that globalisation. They don't know that word: they simply call it death.

I never thought I would see feeding camps in Ethiopia again, but in those twenty years things had got worse. Africa has uniquely grown poorer by 25 per cent. A typical

African country today has the GDP of a town of 20,000 in the UK. Half of its people subsist on 65 pence or less a day. The UN spends $1.3 billion a year on peacekeeping but a fifth of all Africans live in countries riven by civil war. This instability helped spread AIDS which, unknown in 1984, was now killing 6,000 a day. The dead can't plant, so people were starving again. Only one in 400 victims was taking anti-retrovirals. Net investment south of the Sahara was a pathetic $3.9 billion and was worse than in the past six years.

We are all failing Africa but Europe in particular is failing Africa – and itself in the process. I say 'in particular' because they are our immediate neighbour. Our common history goes back millennia – through the black popes and saints, Islamic period, the Crusades, the slave trade and colonialism and post-independence. But it is our future together that is most at stake.

Europe should now stand on the threshold of a great new idea – the ability to lead the planet on a different type of crusade, to make poverty history. It needs to do it, it should do it, and it can do it. It can make the condition of those lives whole and healthy, should it want to. It can, through our example of turning a battered, ruined, bankrupt, starving and war-torn continent into a prosperous and democratic one. And this is the great modern European achievement. The problem is that we have never had a shared sense of the continent's responsibilities to the rest of the world. Each country has gone through its own national rethink, overcoming the knowledge of what we are to the ideal of what we could be: the imperial countries through a mix of naked self-interest and guilt; the Nordics as part of a politically and religiously driven internationalism; the Germans out of historical restitution. And now the EU needs to urgently re-think its fraudulent, inadequate and frankly lying policies on debt, trade and aid.

The Pope enjoined Europe to be open to the other continents. If that is so then Africa makes a mockery of that European ideal. Each of the principles that lie behind the European project – equality, mutuality and solidarity – have been perverted into their opposites: dependence, double standards and duplicity. We drop meagre scraps from our tables of prosperity with one hand, but then scoop them up with the other.

We talk about partnership but we have enslaved a continent with loans – forcing the poorest countries in the world to spend more every year on interest payments than on healthcare and education, and ensuring that all Africans are born into debt slavery and die owing more than when they were born. Some European countries like the Czech Republic, Hungary and Poland have yet to cancel all the debt owed by HIPCs (Heavily Indebted Poor Countries). Other countries like Germany and Italy have promised to do it but not delivered. And many EU states are disgracefully late in paying their contributions to the HIPC Trust Fund for cancelling multilateral debt.

In a nutshell, this reluctance, this tardiness, this grinding unwillingness kills people.

We lecture them on free trade but we close our markets to their agricultural produces and swamp them with subsidised imports of European products. Each European cow gets subsidies worth 157 times what the EU gives to each African. That is actually true: the EU gives €5.4 a year to each person in extreme poverty, it gives €848 a year to each dairy cow in Europe. And even as we talk of making the Doha Round a trade round for development, the French, Greeks, Irish, Italians, Portuguese, Spanish and Poles are continuing to obstruct reform of the Common Agricultural Policy. Our double standards are almost designed to keep Africans in poverty while impoverishing Europe morally. We force them to sell us commodities but prevent them from adding value to them. An African who wants to sell pineapples in the EU faces a tariff of 9 per cent for fresh fruit, 32 per cent for tinned pineapples and 42 per cent for pineapple juice. This goes back to the original perversion of Adam Smith's policies by European colonialists who decided Africa's comparative advantage would be its poverty. Forget the invisible hand of the market: this is the malignant cheating hand of the protection racket that much EU trade regulation is.

Europeans boast loudly that we have bigger aid programmes than anyone else in the world. But over half the money destined by the EU for the world's poorest people is spent in middle income countries, mostly in Europe's immediate neighbourhood. The same is true of many member states: just 6 per cent of Greek aid goes to low-income countries; 15 per cent for Austria; 24 per cent for Finland.

I have worked quite intimately with all the bigger governments. I have thrown up my hands in despair about what they do, what they won't do, and what they pretend they do! Even though all European countries promised twenty-five years ago to increase aid to 0.7 per cent of GDP, the reality is that only four of them have. Italy – the fifth biggest economy in the world – gives only 0.17 per cent!

And worse still, many European countries continue to tie their aid to contracts for their national companies. The money is designed to increase profits rather than reduce poverty. The last survey of aid in Italy showed that 92 per cent of its aid was tied. And over half of Austrian and Spanish aid is tied today.

And European civil society – including the Catholic Church – must also examine its impact on Africa. It is time to go beyond charity, and confront some of the theologically suspect as well as criminally stupid shibboleths that have held back development. Many Christians must have shared Archbishop Tutu's reaction to the nomination of Pope Benedict when he asked him to be 'someone more open to a reasonable position with regards to condoms and HIV/AIDS'.

What makes this so depressing is that it does not have to be this way. The unpalatable truth is that, throughout economic history, those who succeeded economically have nearly always 'kicked away the ladder' beneath them to prevent others from scrambling up behind. That is why today we are imposing so many impossible conditions on poor countries in the form of benign interference, which in truth actually prevent them developing. Perhaps it's not conscious, but this is the manner in which all wealthy countries have always behaved. That's what was so unusual about the United States' Marshall Plan which after the Second World War revived Europe. Yet the reality is that America's genuine legendary generosity was also in its self-interest. The US needed to create a viable trading partner for their uniquely booming post-war economy, a bulwark against the Soviets' threatening Stalinism, and most importantly a philosophical partner giving Europe an absolute identity as part of the West as opposed to turning eastwards.

But today we can put self-interest and European idealism together – because through our wealth the end of extreme poverty is genuinely within our grasp. We need to develop our own version of the Marshall Plan for Africa – showing the same sense of foresight and idealism that America showed in our own continent. It is not just that an Africa freed from the yoke of extreme poverty will be less of a security threat. In the 1960s, South Korea had a GDP per capita the same size as Nigeria, and look at how our economies and societies have benefited from the rise of Asia.

The potential is there. I have spent time with Gordon Brown and Tony Blair and I can tell that, while their eyes glaze over in European Council meetings, they light up when the subject turns to Africa. In Africa we find a focus to the latent common idealism of the continent which allows European citizens to make a common cause with their political leaders – a solidarity of concern that can be matched by a solidarity of self-interest at the bureaucratic level. This is a unique year to talk about these issues: in the UK we have a concurrency of presidencies, that of the G8 and the EU, and coincidentally the twentieth anniversary of Live Aid. And what is more than that – we do have a plan.

I have learnt in the last twenty years that it is no longer appropriate to deal with each of the African issues on an individual basis. Debt, trade, aid, AIDS, war, hunger: these are merely the individual excrescences of the singular condition that is poverty. Even here, no matter how vast the lobby, the momentary enthusiasm for one campaign leads rapidly to public boredom and the focus changes to the next conundrum. I was involved in the Drop the Debt issue, a hugely successful public lobby to deal with the laceratingly cruel, ridiculous and immoral debt slavery into which we had pushed the continent. The troops were summoned, banners raised, the unions and churches sounded the clarion cry of Middle England, that greatest of political lobbies, the Pope pronounced and – presto – a third of debt was wiped out, to no obvious discomfort to us, but equally, as it turned out, to not much gain to them. A little bit, in some countries, sure, but in general new acronyms and devices were implemented for us to hide behind and pretend we were doing something but also making countries who could never pay, who produced less than their debt burden, leap through ever more arcane financial hoops and hurdles.

Earlier this year, the Africa Commission, of which I was a member, produced a comprehensive report that looked at how we can move from a piecemeal approach to a blueprint for ending extreme poverty in Africa. We held consultations in forty-nine individual countries across Africa, in every G8 country, throughout Europe, and China. We received nearly 500 formal submissions and examined the vast wealth of analysis on aid and development over the past fifty years. Our lessons confirm some of Europe's deepest experiences – and show that we can be part of the solution, rather than the problem.

The most important conclusion is that the one factor underlying all sub-Saharan Africa's difficulties over the past forty years is the weakness of governance and the absence of an effective state.

It was Africa's misfortune not only to have been plundered by Europe, but also to have been colonised at a time when the concept of the nation state was firmly entrenched as a primary determinant of the historical process. The consequence is that today the continent is divided into forty-six states, more than three times the number of Asia (whose land mass is 50 per cent larger), and nearly four times the number of South America. More states are entirely land-locked in Africa – fifteen – than in the rest of the world put together, and no country in Africa is free from problems of access, security and economic stability that is directly attributable to the boundaries they inherited from the colonial era.

But the one common feature that unites many of these states is that they don't work. That is why one of the Commission's main recommendations was to make a major investment to improve Africa's capacity, that is the means and structures that enable administrations to govern by working through the building of systems and staff in local and national governments, but also in trans-national bodies such as the African Union and the ten regional economic communities that are developing in west, east, central and southern Africa.

Effective states need accountability. Like the EU, African governments have to ensure that their systems are open to the scrutiny of their citizens. That means strengthening parliaments, the media, trade unions and the judiciary. Rich nations also have the responsibility to stop corruption. As Mobutu, the unlamented thug who looted Zaire into paralysis, said, 'It takes two to corrupt; the corrupter and the corrupted.' They must track down money looted from Africa, now sitting in foreign bank accounts, and send that money back to those from whom it was stolen. Western banks must be obliged by law to inform on suspicious accounts. As in Europe, those who give bribes must be tackled as well as those who take them. Foreign companies, especially those in the oil and mining industries, must be pressed to publish what they pay to governments. And firms who bribe should be refused export credits.

Above all, in a continent of thousands of ethnicities where, in contrast to the Europe which invented it, the nation state has never really taken root, we need to support Africa's attempts to build a Union for their continent like the European Union. Indeed it is conceivable that Africa needs it more than Europe. When a citizen perceives no benefit from the state he will look to give his loyalties elsewhere, in Africa's case to the clan or tribe and, more recently, to Islam in the North and Evangelical Christianity in the South. This can be seen to be an attempt to join in a supra-national overarching entity transcending the narrow confines of the failed state. In this way Africans gain purchase on a form of globalised power. They have always understood that spiritual power is political power, something that we in Europe are having to re-discover to our dismay. I leave it to you to decide if this is a good thing or not. Either way it's a reality.

Africa is confronted by shameful trade barriers that tax

its goods as they enter the markets of the rich world. These must be dismantled. But African nations do not trade between themselves. A mere 12 per cent of all African goods go to other African countries. Africans must reduce and simplify the tariff systems between one African country and another. It must reform excessive bureaucracy, cumbersome customs procedures, and corruption by public servants. It must make it easier to set up businesses. It must improve the way African nations work with one another in the continent's regional economic communities.

So what can Europe do? Trade justice. Drop the debt. More and better aid. We must draw deep down on our history of building effective states, investing in infrastructure, supporting democratic transitions and regional economic integration.

One of the things that unites the European club is our smugness. But if there is one challenge I want to set Europe it is to live up to its rhetoric. Everyone likes to attack George Bush – but when it comes to Africa we don't have that much to be smug about. The US starts from a very low base, but in the last few years he has doubled aid to Africa, introduced the Millennium Challenge Account involving billions of dollars, and is giving $3 billion a year to the fight against AIDS. He challenged Europe to respond – but then nothing happened. If people want Europe to balance America, I'll give you a cause. Let's match that record and lead where we know others will follow, in the alleviation of the greatest moral sore and potentially dangerous political problem at the beginning of the twenty-first century: the grotesque impoverishment of an entire continent; the annual mass dying of those who have nothing.

The cost of the Commission's whole package of proposals would be an extra $75 billion a year. Africa can pay for about a third of this if we open our markets to them and let them trade. The rest must financed by increases in aid. Aid should be doubled now, from $25 billion a year to $50 billion. Though this sounds a lot, it is the work of moments to achieve and something we have always promised but never done. We must also end negative aid, which is what debt repayments constitute. That means 100 per cent cancellation of Africa's debts to institutions such as the IMF and World Bank. The amounts involved are large, the equivalent of a Marshall Plan for Africa, but the costs to Europeans would be tiny (just 10p in every £100 we earn). And look at what we would gain: ending the tyranny of extreme poverty that sees 8 million people die every year because they are too poor to stay alive; stopping 15,000 people a day from death at the hands of AIDS, TB and malaria; giving all boys and girls free primary education; empowering women; reducing child mortality. And as Europeans we would have an African neighbour that is not a security threat, and a new market on our doorstep with hundreds of millions of potential consumers. And by helping Africa, we might find even ourselves as Europeans gaining an identity in the same way that the West did through the Marshall Plan, but this time for Europe through the Blair Plan.

People say that there are no great causes left. The original generation of Europeans had a big cause: the end of war. Their successors embarked on the necessary – if unglamorous process – of putting the European economy back together again, a process that ended with the creation of the single European market and the single currency. Finally, last year, we ended the third phase of European integration: spreading democracy to Eastern Europe and creating a Europe that is whole and free.

The next phase of building Europe cannot just be about passing constitutions, meeting the Lisbon targets or developing new types of regulation. We need a European project that can inspire Europe's people. Closing the gap between European values and our role in the world must be that project. Europe's citizens can believe in it. Europe's leaders must now live up to these values. We can find solidarity among ourselves through our commitment to the world. And this movement can start here today, in London, the capital of the country that will host the G8 summit and the European presidency for the second half of the year. The presidency that could Make Poverty History, and unite Europe not just theoretically, not negatively, not bureaucratically, economically or politically but idealistically, emotionally, spiritually into an elevated sense of ourselves.

EUROPE IN SOLIDARITY

Not the narrow negative solidarity of meanness, nor the thin join of imposed union; not the odious odes to ersatz joy but a great European US in a solidarity of justice, of value, a solidarity of the European soul.

5 Europe in the Wider World
Lord Patten of Barnes CH

I begin with a confession, not the first I have made in this great brick basilica, which used to be my parish church, but certainly the first in public. Here it is. I have never confused an election campaign with a Socratic dialogue. We are not witnesses, as the weeks of electioneering drag past, to a reflective hunt for the truth. I take my share of the blame. I was once – 'autres temps, autres moeurs' – guilty of mangling Shakespeare's language in the pursuit of votes. It is sad to reflect that a politician, Adlai Stevenson, who exemplified as well as any the attempt to raise the level of political debate, coining the phrase that 'the average man is a great deal better than the average', lost two Presidential elections. So it is difficult to recall a campaign that appealed to the reflective side of our natures, that urged us to think of the long term and of broader horizons.

Old hack that I am, even I was surprised by the things that went undiscussed in our recent electoral capers. There seemed at times to be an informal conspiracy to keep some subjects off the air, and certainly off the *Today* programme, however hard its producers might have rightly tried to disoblige the political rivals. Admittedly, thanks to lobbying by development organisations, there was a Sunday when all the party leaders made reverential speeches about world poverty. They were against it. But while we heard about school dinners and matrons, and nothing wrong with that, I recall no discussion of the relationship between national energy choices and environmental hazard or the impact of demography on social policy. It was not until the week after polling day that we heard some thoughtful remarks by Adair Turner on this subject. Nor of course was anything said during the campaign about Europe; as an electoral issue it was never 'outed'. It has been left to Cardinal Cormac's series of lectures to recognise how many serious issues there are to debate on Europe. I have not agreed with all that I have read in the previous excellent lectures. But their content, and the size of the audiences for them, does suggest an interest that has gone unmet elsewhere.

What makes the collective political vow of *omertà* on this subject so strange is that the tone of argument about Europe when debate is actually joined, for example in Mr Murdoch's newspapers, suggests that the issues go right to the heart of our national identity and national interest. The glorious independence of our island home is about to be subverted; our customs and constitution – unwritten and sometimes unfathomable though it may be – are to be extinguished by Johnny Foreigner. No more Queen, no more Wall's sausages. On the other side of the argument, the European Union – this extraordinary, imperfect, ramshackle but still working enterprise in sovereignty sharing – is sometimes spoken about in terms that suggest that it has been handed down from the gods, not stuck together by man, one compromise spatchcocked onto another. To question it or Britain's role in it is impious, a liberal apostasy frowned on in polite society.

I suppose the principal excuse given for Hamlet's absence from the play – or maybe it was the grave-diggers who failed to show up – is that we have been promised a referendum, or to be more accurate two referenda on aspects of this debate, the constitutional treaty and our willingness or otherwise to join the eurozone. I hate referenda, the favourite electoral device of tabloid editors. I hate them precisely because of what they do to parliamentary democracy at Westminster. If the issues that they are to determine are so important, they should decide who forms the government of this country. The fact that we try to sideline them, channelling them into a different electoral process, helps to make the discussion of them as ignorantly rabid as it is.

Well, we are alas where we are, though whether we ever have a referendum on the constitutional treaty and a serious debate on the issues it raises, is entirely dependent on others – specifically, President Chirac and the French electorate. So much for British democracy. 'Non' means 'no' to the treaty and to any British debate. I suppose we had all better keep our powder dry in case the result is a 'oui', and I would not wish by pre-empting future arguments to be accused of pulpit abuse. But it really is a rum old world.

I owe it to you to indicate the encasement of opinions or prejudices about the EU out of which my remarks this evening will seek to clamber. First, I believe that the European idea, which I will try in part to illuminate, is perhaps inevitably better than the institutions that serve it and better, too, than many of the arguments adduced in its favour. Second, this is partly because the EU, like the United Nations, is a clanking man-made institution, struggling away to cross the muddy terrain between reality and aspiration. To say that it is imperfect is not to say it is wrong and that we should have nothing to do with it. The system of Westminster democracy and Cabinet government can feel like an awful let-down when you are part of it. I cannot speak for the Vatican. Third, there is an insularity about our own discussion of our relationship to Europe that is only matched by the continental introversion of Europe, made all the more obvious as India and China re-emerge as great world powers. If we want to help shape the future, do we think that we can do it on our own – 'this is Britain calling' – or as America's loyal side-kick, an adjutant occasionally allowed to speak up politely in the mess, or as part of a continent that makes far too little of its collective influence and is too fixated at present on its own internal affairs? What should be the main items on our agenda as Europeans – twenty-five nation states – in seeking to ensure a more powerful, stable and prosperous world? Like Caesar's Gaul, I divide the task into three.

First, the excesses of European nationalism helped to make the world in the first half of the last century less peaceful, less stable and less prosperous. Out of the economic and political rivalry of those nation states largely created in the previous century, came war, ruin, division and tyranny. That was the rubble 'in death's grey land' out of which, with American help and encouragement, we began to build today's Europe, with at its heart France and Germany lashed together in a historic reconciliation. A difference between modern Europe and Asia is that there has been no similar reconciliation in the East between China and Japan. From the outset the European Union, whose different names – from market to community to union – reflect the steady achievement of its sequential objectives, was a profoundly political project in which economic means were used to achieve political purposes. One of them was the creation of a neighbourhood of prosperous, stable democracies trading freely with one another. So characteristically when Spain, Portugal and Greece escaped the bonds of authoritarianism, they were immediately offered membership of the Union to consolidate their democracy and to invigorate their economies. The same approach governed our attitude to the European countries from which we were separated by the barbed wire of the Cold War and the Soviet Empire. As the USSR and the Warsaw Pact crumbled, Europe's policy was to offer membership of our Union to the countries that Russia had colonised. Paradoxically for some people, countries like Poland and Hungary celebrated the recovery of their national independence by proposing the earliest possible sharing of much of their newly regained sovereignty with others.

Enlargement of the EU was the most successful foreign policy that Europe has implemented. It was the policy for our own backyard, our own neighbourhood, and it worked. Only in the Balkans was the dismemberment of the last European empire accompanied by bloodshed; elsewhere prospering, plural democracies flourish from Lisbon to – almost – Lviv. But that raises a tough question for us, one that I want to consider. Where should our boundaries now lie? Why, for example, is Lviv on the wrong side of the line? Each enlargement produces a new neighbourhood. Do we extend the EU until we get to the Pacific's shores? When and where do we stop?

Obviously, increasing the size of the EU puts political and institutional strains on its policies and programmes. A Union of six member states is very different to one of twenty-five, and that in turn is different to one of thirty-five. As the Union has grown, it has changed already, and so it should. There is no reason why the institutions at Europe's heart should stay exactly the same until the crack of doom, and that indeed is in part what the constitutional treaty attempts to deal with. We do need to be clearer about what has to be done at the European level and what at the national. The budget, the regional funds, the Common Agricultural Policy are also all affected by enlargement, and there would be few tears outside the Elysée Palace if one consequence of enlargement was a final radical overhaul of the way we try to assist poor farmers, rural development and the protection of our European countryside. So it is no answer to the question of the delineation of the EU's boundaries to claim the sanctity either of existing methods of governance or of present policy.

In the founding treaties of the EU, the criteria that need to be satisfied to qualify for negotiating membership are very simple. Is the country concerned European, and does it share Europe's values? If a country passes those simple tests, demonstrating that it embraces pluralist democratic values under the rule of law in a genuine, not merely ceremonial or bogus way, then we have no right to deny it a place at the negotiating table. The negotiations may not succeed, but they should certainly start.

Not all our neighbours can satisfy these tests. For them – the countries on the southern and eastern Mediterranean shore, and the countries of the Southern Caucasus, for example – we have devised another policy, under which we seek to negotiate binding contractual agreements that should enable them in time to share our markets and many of our policies, and to share too our commitment to pluralism and democracy, without becoming members of the Union.

But there are three examples of countries that in my judgement cannot be denied the perspective of EU membership without us resiling from the principle of creating a stable and democratic neighbourhood to which we have for so long been committed.

First, there are the countries of South-east Europe including the Western Balkans. Two of these countries – Romania and Bulgaria – are already promised entry into the EU in 2007. I remain concerned that this date is too ambitious, especially for Romania. But I shall be content to be proved wrong, and at least the Romanians now have a government that is serious about tackling corruption. Albania and the countries that were once part of the now dismembered Yugoslavia are already promised membership one day; Croatia and Macedonia are in the initial stages of negotiation. There are two issues that cast long shadows over the whole region. The first is whether it can escape its own recent history, admitting the crimes done in the name of ethnicity and nationalism, and co-operating fully with the international community to bring those responsible for war crimes to justice. I believe that the Catholic Church has played at best a mixed role in promoting reconciliation in the Balkans. The leadership of the Cardinal Archbishop of Vienna has been exemplary, not least in relation to the Islamic communities in the region. But I would have difficulty saying the same about the Church in Croatia, parts of which seem to have a real difficulty distinguishing between Catholicism and revanchist nationalism.

The second shadow is organised crime. We do not take it sufficiently seriously. Nor do the countries in the region. They tell us what they are doing to stamp it out. We pretend to believe them. We have to be more open in raising our concerns. The victims of our coyness are the young girls who are pressed into prostitution in our cities, the drug addicts on our streets, and the poor urban communities terrorised by well-organised gangs.

To the East of the present EU, bordering Poland, Hungary and Slovakia, lies the country whose name means 'borderland', Ukraine. This is a country whose frontiers have frequently changed as dynasties, nations and armies have tramped this way and that across the Carpathian mountains and the steppes between the Dniester and Dnieper rivers. Is Ukraine geographically part of Europe? Yes. Is it historically and culturally part of Europe? Yes to that question too – especially its Western half. Do its aspirations lie with Europe? Remember the scenes of those crowds in Kiev sporting their orange flags and favours. What do we say to those Europeans who have risked all for democracy? Are we to tell them that the club is full, but that we wish them well in their efforts to sustain democracy, in the lee of a bruised and brooding Russia? And if we take in Ukraine, how can we ignore Moldova, a country literally crippled by Russia's cynical refusal to help resolve the problem of Transnistria? However hard and imaginatively we work to stabilise our neighbourhood, we find ourselves running into a serious difference of opinion with Russia, a difference that our political leaders are reluctant to face squarely. The EU believe that the countries of our region should be strong, independent and prosperous. Russia does not want strong and independent neighbours: Russia today wants pliable neighbours in a sphere of influence. The Tsars wished for the same. Views that we developed in Western Europe in the second half of the twentieth century clash with views that dominated that century's earliest bloody years.

Turkey's position is different still. Since Ataturk Turkey has claimed a place in Europe, a point that was conceded forty-two years ago when the President of the European Commission, Walter Hallstein, signed an Association Agreement with Turkey, declaring when he did so, 'Turkey is part of Europe. This is the deepest possible meaning of this operation which brings, in the most appropriate way conceivable in our time, the confirmation of a geographical reality as well as a historical truism that has been valid for several centuries.' In those days the military and the security services dominated Turkish politics. Today Turkey is a democracy, so much so that the then American Deputy Secretary of Defence, Paul Wolfowitz, was despatched to Ankara after the Iraq invasion to scold the generals there for not having pushed their elected government into allowing American forces to attack Iraq from Turkey in the north. This is the same Turkey that America often and rightly presses us to accept as an EU member.

We are told that this question of Turkish membership feeds negative sentiment about the constitutional treaty in the referendum campaigns in France and the Netherlands. It does so, I suspect, for reasons that will help determine what Europe is to become. There are worries about uncontrolled migration from deepest rural Anatolia. But Turkish entry to the EU does not need to mean that if – even in demographic free fall – we do not want it. Second, and more significant, there is a sense that our identity as Europeans is threatened by the arrival in the Union of an Islamic state. How so? We were not yesterday and are not today a society in Europe that can define itself coterminously with the Christian faith. Are we to deny the role of Jews and Muslims in our political, artistic, scientific, literary, commercial and architectural history? Are we to overlook the African and Asian roots of Christianity itself? Maybe it is true that we live in a largely secular society today, albeit with Christian roots and with – as Timothy Radcliffe argued – a deep spiritual want. But for all its casual, puzzled agnosticism, it is also a pretty tolerant society, and Turkey's accession to the EU would enable us to demonstrate that tolerance at home and in the wider world.

Over a decade ago, the American political scientist Samuel Huntingdon wrote an influential book which predicted that the triumph of liberal democracy in Europe and the collapse of Communism would not be followed by global peace, a landscape dominated by lions lying down with lambs, but by a clash of civilisations: Confucian, Islamic, Christian. I argued strongly against that idea, which was used in Asia to justify authoritarianism, as though there was some cultural hostility in Confucianism to pluralism, human rights and democracy. The Asian financial crash of 1997–9 seemed to justify the sort of arguments that people like me had put forward; authoritarianism and crony capitalism did not represent either the Confucian tradition or the way of the future. Recovery from financial ruin often involved – for example in Thailand and South Korea – political as well as economic reform, transparency as well as better regulation. Then came the manifestations of Islamic political extremism in the 2000s, above all the atrocities in New York and Washington, and it seemed again that Huntingdon might be correct.

We sometimes seem to have been trying, in much of what the Western world has done or has failed to do in the years since September 2001, to make Huntingdon's predictions come true. Turkey's accession to the EU would work in the opposite direction. It would enable Europe to throw a bridge across the fissures between the West and Islam, to show that democracy, tolerance and pluralism can prosper in Islamic societies as in Western. Turkey has been doing all

71

the things that we urge on other Islamic countries in the name of democracy and human rights. What are other Islamic countries to conclude about us if, even after all this, we still judge that Turkey cannot join our club? What reason would we give that would sound even passingly plausible? If we want Western Asia to be democratic and stable, the best way of achieving that aim is by embracing the Islamic democracy that stands on the cusp between Europe and Asia.

A stable, peaceful continent was the first of the principles that determined our development and that of our neighbours; the second principle we applied was trying to resolve our arguments through a rules-based system for settling these disputes. This is what underpins the day-to-day functioning of the EU. We used to fight for Strasbourg, now we argue there (and in Brussels and Luxembourg), argue and haggle about quotas for this and standards for that, a preferable and more civilised way for neighbours to do business than any previously tried or immediately obvious alternative. Some smart commentators call it postmodern. I would myself drop the 'post'. There are two essential elements in this pooling of sovereignty. The first is that it is a delusion for nation states to think that they can handle the problems or grasp the opportunities that crowd in on them on their own. Stand aside from sharing the taking of decisions with others, and you retain all the sovereignty that comes from not having a say in the decisions that others will in any event take, decisions that directly affect you. The second element is that the system only works if the rules apply equally to all. Of course, this does not reflect the fact that the bigger you are the more you are likely to be able to shape the rules that everyone has to follow. But 'you' – however big you may be – are part of the 'everyone'.

I suppose the best example of this approach outside our own borders was the American leadership in the creation of the institutions of global governance after the Second World War. America was the global super-power, only challenged by the sinister designs of Stalin's Soviet Union. The old empires were in retreat, if not collapse. Self-determination was the order of the day. From the war-time Atlantic

Charter onwards, America sought to create agencies and rules that would provide the framework for dragging the world out of chaos into prosperous pluralism. The UN was established, then the Bretton Woods institutions and the forerunner of the WTO. The Declaration of Human Rights was agreed, with Eleanor Roosevelt leading the charge. Work began in the wake of the trials in Nuremburg and Tokyo to establish an international court to try future crimes against humanity – and, hey presto, in fifty years we have one. But what was this? In the 2000s America opposed its establishment. This is not a continuation of past policy, any more than the present American stance on global warming and climate change reflects the continuation of opposition to environmental diplomacy. As recently as the 1980s it was America that was pressing often reluctant Europeans to accept the precautionary principle in environmental policy; it was America that was then leading the search to find ways of involving developing countries in environmental agreements whose present requirement was the result of the past practices of developed countries but whose future efficacy would demand the compliance of today's developing economies. That was what happened with the prohibition on ozone-depleting substances in the 1980s. Unlike other mighty powers, America did not by and large seek to turn its strength into territorial acquisition or a selfish disregard for the interests of the rest of the world; it led the creation of a global network of rules, and mostly accepted them for itself. America's much applauded soft power exceeded the explosive potential of the content of all its silos. It could change regimes with its tanks and marines; but, more important, it could change societies through its example.

At a time when we most need effective global co-operation to deal with global threats – from terrorism to environmental calamity to nuclear proliferation – some American sovereigntists question the very idea of an international rule of law and the role of the UN to prevent conflict and to legitimise the use of force when conflict is unavoidable. Indeed it is proposed to send a leading sovereigntist to New York to represent America at the UN there. What should Europe do? First, we have to do all we can to make the international system work better, though its effectiveness will be limited if America contracts out of international initiatives and agreements. In order to improve the prospects of consensus on the present proposals for UN reform, Europe should speak as one in supporting them. Second, we should accept explicitly that sometimes the preservation of the international rule of law requires the use of force, or its threatened use. To the extent that we flinch from this unfortunate truth, we lower our credibility in American eyes, living up to the caricature that Europe talks softly and carries a big carrot. Third, where America for the time being has contracted out of global agreements, for example the Kyoto Protocol and the International Criminal Court, we shall have to carry the responsibility for attempting to make them work. I do not believe that the present passage in American policy represents a permanent rejection of the interests of the rest of the world and the way of managing global affairs that America above all others created. But to persuade America to return to a different path, Europe has to speak and act convincingly as one – as a partner and friend, but not a rival.

An immediate challenge for Europe is how to prevent the proliferation of nuclear weapons. The existing arrangements, policed by the International Atomic Energy Agency, have not worked too badly. There are today eight nuclear powers; President Kennedy used to fear that there could by now be two or three times that number. But we are faced today with a real threat of the disintegration of the existing arrangements. North Korea may well already have nuclear weapons; Iran declines to abandon the potential capacity to manufacture them. How should the world react? What is required – with America and China taking the lead in the case of North Korea, and Europe and America in the case of Iran – is a tough and coherent policy in each case that combines inducements with the threat of sanctions. But if sanctions are to be credible, we need to be sure that if and when we go to the UN Security Council to get endorsement for them, we receive its approval. Here we run into a difficulty created by an all-too obvious example of double standards. The Nuclear Non-Proliferation Treaty, whose provisions are currently under review, needs to be tightened in order to reduce the capacity of non-nuclear powers to go nuclear. But they are reluctant to accept new and tougher obligations on their own side when the existing nuclear powers seem reluctant to accept their existing obligations to get rid of more of their own weapons and to abandon the development of a future generation of nuclear munitions. The main problem here is America's reluctance to forgo any future research, development or testing of nuclear weapons, or to forswear any first use of nuclear weapons against a non-nuclear state. If we need to get tough with Iran or North Korea, then we must convince other countries that the rich well-armed West is prepared to play by the rules it wants them to accept.

Our third principle in Europe is that our own societies should be plural democracies respecting human rights under the rule of law, and that these values should be reflected in our external policies. This is what is sometimes rather lumpishly called having an ethical foreign policy. I have never really understood the arguments that have raged around this idea. First, it seems fairly obvious that it is better to have an explicitly ethical than an unethical foreign policy. 'What are the aims of your policy, Minister?' 'Well, I want to act as immorally as possible around the world.' It doesn't sound quite right, does it? Second, on the other hand to go around bragging that your every act is infused with a higher morality runs the risk of upset as the best of intentions bark their shins against the reality of a naughty world. Optimists like me believe in original virtue, but we still have to concede that it has to co-exist with original sin. Third – and this is a point that the Victorians used to express in their hymns – it is normally good sense to try to do the right thing. In my experience, there is a remarkable correlation in making policy between expedience and morality. Democracies make the best neighbours. The safest countries in which to invest are the ones that treat their citizens decently. The law for Citizen 'X' is the same as the law for Ronald McDonald. Stability and democracy are most likely to be found where people have full stomachs.

Let me begin these final remarks with this proposition, though I will not labour a point that featured prominently in Bob Geldof's lecture and on which there is broad agreement. Giving hungry people lectures on democracy is unlikely to bring much success in transforming their own attitudes and those of the societies in which they struggle to exist. Europe is the biggest aid donor in the world and is committed to doing much better. For years while a virtuous handful of northern European countries achieved the 0.7 per cent UN target, most of us piously expressed a commitment to it while in practice the target disappeared over a distant horizon. I think it was Harold Wilson who once drew a distinction between a pledge and a lightly given promise. For too long, on aid we have been in the lightly-given-promise department. In real terms, aid budgets fell. Now we have turned the corner and done so in a way that promises to make easily verifiable progress. More European countries have now committed themselves to target dates for reaching 0.7 per cent. In addition, the EU's older member states have agreed a succession of steps, with all achieving the EU average figure by given dates, which will ratchet up individual programmes with the European aggregate rising as they do so. Each time the average increases, it will drag up individual programmes. It does not help the starving when the aid debate turns into developed countries arguing over decimal points of percentages to show their allegedly greater generosity to the poor. But I was surprised by Bob Geldof's extremely charitable remarks about America's record. One day I hope that America's 0.15 per cent will overtake Italy's almost equally lamentable figure.

It is a cliché, though nevertheless true, that trade is more important than aid; if Africa, for example, was able to recover half the share of global exports that it enjoyed two decades ago, the result would be worth many times any conceivable increase in aid flow. The Doha Trade Round must achieve what it was advertised to do, namely to make the world's trade rules fairer to the poor, to open American, Japanese and European markets wider to the agricultural produce of developing countries, and to stop dumping subsidised food on world markets. The next head of the WTO, the admirable Pascal Lamy, knows all this, as does his successor as EU Trade Commissioner, Peter Mandelson.

They need and deserve all our political support to make it happen.

Trade and aid will not by themselves produce that elusive higher growth in poor countries without better governance. Developing countries themselves have to show a strong commitment to this. The declared African covenant on democracy, the rule of law and human rights alas failed one of its earliest tests in Zimbabwe.

Around the globe, Europe seeks to show its determination to support the broadening of participative government and an improvement in human rights by attaching clauses covering these issues to the trade and co-operation agreements we sign with other countries. This has been a particular feature of our partnership with Arab countries around the Mediterranean. I would not raise questions about this approach if we took it more seriously. But beyond the occasional European *démarche* – which does not exactly make strong men tremble – we have done little to stand over the contractual nature of human rights clauses. Today, we are in the ridiculous position of having human rights agreements with countries in the Middle East to which the present American administration sends suspected terrorists under the Orwellian-named policy of 'extraordinary rendition' to be interrogated according to their own local methods – methods that have been all too well documented in the reports of Amnesty International and Human Rights Watch.

Far better in my view than negotiating these well-meaning but toothless clauses would be to set aside a much larger proportion of co-operation budgets for those countries that meet specific goals set by themselves but agreed with Europe and other donors for improving governance and the protection of human rights. Positive conditionality – rewarding good behaviour – is in practice much easier to manage than taking benefits away from those who behave badly.

A stable and democratic neighbourhood, support for the international rule of law and the institutions that seek to monitor it, and the pursuit of values in external policy – these seem to me to provide the right framework for Europe's policy in the wider world. 'If men could learn from history,' lamented Samuel Coleridge, 'what lessons it might teach us. But passion and party blind our eyes, and the light which experience gives us is a lantern on the stern which shines only on the waves behind us.' The image is compelling and beautiful, but the message is actually wrong. Seeing the state of the sea behind us gives us at least some idea of what the sea will be like ahead. That is what has informed the creation of the European Union, and the principles that it seeks to follow in its relations with the wider world. We may be maladroit; we may promise more than we achieve; we may from time to time stand accused of hypocrisy and double standards. Saints we are not. But I think that what we glean in the dark from the light on the stern, what we learn from our own history, is a valuable guide to present and future policy, and I only hope that we can follow that guidance more boldly and faithfully in the years ahead.

6 The Church in Europe

Cardinal Cormac Murphy-O'Connor

The shape of the Church now

It seems an age now, but it was only a few weeks ago that
with the other 113 cardinals I came out onto the balcony
overlooking St Peter's Square alongside Pope Benedict.
Just half an hour before, we had chosen him, under God, to
be the shepherd of our global flock, the visible focus of
unity of our billion-strong faith. What a crowd! Half a million people had rushed into the square as the news flashed
around the world that white smoke had gushed from the
chimney above the Sistine Chapel. It was the final act in a
series of dramas, beginning with the suffering and death of
John Paul II, which for three weeks had held the world
transfixed. What marvels the Lord performed in that time.
We will not easily forget them. No wonder that among
Pope Benedict's first public utterances were those ringing
words, 'The Church is alive!'

That is certainly what we saw from that balcony. And
what was running through my head, as that immense
crowd roared its joy at our new Peter, was how far we have
come since the Holy Spirit of Pentecost blew into the Upper
Room in Jerusalem. As I stood, two thousand years dis-
solved at that moment into a single instant – and I thought,
*what a journey we, the Church, have been on since God's love
was first poured into those first disciples.* And I thought, too, of
the hope there is for our future.

We had elected a wise and holy pastor, a German from the
heartland of our old continent whose culture is impregnated
with Christianity like no other. Both he, and the name he
took, carry great resonances for the history of our Church's
pilgrimage in Europe. St Benedict is the co-patron of Europe
whose Rule for monks in the early Middle Ages was the
light that streamed through our Dark Ages. In the 1700s,
Benedict XIV confronted the scepticism and rationalism of

the Enlightenment. And Benedict XV was the great bridge-builder, who between 1914 and 1922 was the still, small voice of compassion and peace in a continent that was tearing itself apart in hatred and violence, war and revolution.

And while all this was going on in Rome, our lecture series here in the cathedral had begun. What a treat it has been. When I first contemplated this lecture series just over two years ago, one of my inspirations was the exhortation of John Paul II, *Ecclesia in Europa*. I am delighted that the series has, by providential timing, been a kind of bridge between the death of John Paul II, who came out of the Eastern side of a Europe divided by an iron curtain, and the election of Benedict XVI, who said he had taken his name in part because of his special concern for Europe.

Ecclesia in Europa exhorts us to relive our roots; to be again what we are. 'For the most urgent matter Europe faces,' John Paul II said, 'is a growing need of hope, a hope that will enable us to give meaning to life and history, and to continue on our way together.' Pope John Paul knew that Europe and Christianity are not coterminous; that the building blocks of our culture are varied; that today Europe is at a crossroads of pluralism, of different faiths and none. But he also understood that Europe has a soul, a soul imbued by the Christian faith, and that the neglect of that soul is shrivelling our continent to the detriment of all. That is why John Paul invited us all to take stock, again, of our home, to dust off the crucifixes, to escape for a time from the clamour and hear again the still, small voices deep in our European souls. That is what this lecture series has been about and I imagine, with what I hope is legitimate pride, John Paul will be happy at the enthusiasm with which we have accepted his invitation, at the depth and wisdom of our speakers, at the range of issues we have covered.

Jean Vanier, that prophet of the discarded, was our first speaker. His l'Arche communities of people with special needs are to today's Europe what Benedict's monasteries were to earlier centuries: schools of love and acceptance, hearths of hospitality in which ideas of the good and the beautiful are overturned. Jean was speaking just after the funeral of Pope John Paul. Those days were an incredible sign of hope, a witness, Jean said, greater than any encyclical John Paul II wrote, for he had showed us what it means to die with grit and grace, as the good shepherd who gives his life for his flock.

Europe has achieved great things, as President Mary McAleese reminded us. 'In the debris of the dismal first half of twentieth century Europe, a group of men and women consciously decided to try love and not hate, to put into radical action the great commandment to love one another,' she told us. But 'Europe is an infant still . . . in need of care, nourishment and protection if it is to reach proper maturity,' she went on, noting, as so many of our speakers have done, that 'we will only discover a true and rooted European identity in openness and solidarity towards other peoples.' She cast a gaze across the symptoms of hopelessness in our continent, our declining birth rate, our suicides, our addictions, our rages, our lonely elderly, the manifold symptoms of our sense of meaninglessness. Perhaps, she suggested, we need to look again into that abyss from which the European project was born, to remind ourselves of our wounds.

Our third speaker, Fr Timothy Radcliffe, one of our country's greatest preachers, has already told us how Europe is today a place of believing without belonging. Beneath the suburban complacency which has dulled Europe there is a restlessness, a searching, a longing; and these are expressed in the extraordinary popularity of pilgrimages and retreats alongside churches which are sometimes empty. Fr Timothy said this was the task of the Church in contemporary Europe – to 'travel with people as they search for the good, the true and the beautiful'.

Our consciences were stung, too, by Sir Bob Geldof, who looked at Europe from the eyes of Africa. Europe, he said, feels empty, a Milton Keynes continent of Pooterish ambition, in which technocracy and introversion have produced a blind smugness which allows our leaders to give our cows 157 times more in subsidies than what the EU gives to each African. If the European project is again to inspire Europe's people, he told us, we must find solidarity among ourselves again by feeding our souls, rather than our egos, through service to the poorest in the world.

Lord Patten only last week reinforced this message by

inviting the European Union itself to expand, to become broad and generous, to offer a global framework for dragging the world out of chaos into prosperous pluralism, by re-emphasising human rights.

I want to thank our speakers for summoning us all to our roots, for allowing us, over these weeks, to realise again who we are, just as the Church has again woken these past weeks to what it is – God's gift to humanity, a place of transformation, a school of human flourishing. If Europe is to become what we all know in our hearts it must be, it needs the Church, as never before, to help it to do this.

The future shape of the Church

My challenge tonight is to explain *how* it might do this, and what shape it will need for that task. That means understanding some of the questions of our time: questions about the deepest and most profound aspects of the way we live and the purpose of our life – the questions that are borne in our hearts occasionally like aching wounds. What is to become of me? What does my life mean? Where am I bound with my baggage of pain, consolation and joy?

These questions must be the Church's too, as the first words of Second Vatican Council's document on the Church in the modern world make clear. They are the words which I took as my episcopal motto, *Gaudium et Spes*. That document opens with these immortal lines: 'The joy and hope, the grief and anguish of the people of our time, especially of those who are poor or afflicted in any way, are the joy and hope, the grief and anguish of the followers of Christ too.'

But how is the Church to take on the world's joys and griefs, in a more secular Europe? Now secularism is not in itself antagonistic to the Church. There is both a secularism that is neutral and a secularism which is aggressive. The second does not acknowledge the proper separation of temporal and spiritual, Church and State, but is hostile to the legitimate presence of the Church, and so sets out to eliminate God and his Church from playing its role in civic and social formation. It is this aggressive secularism, which make so many – including Pope Benedict – feel wary.

But the response to aggressive secularism cannot be

aggressive Christianity. Remember the contrast between Babel and Pentecost. The Tower of Babel was built by pious people who wanted to make a name for themselves, inspired by the will for power and self-assertion; they wanted to build a temple to God, in the name of God, but not for God. Pentecost reversed the disaster of Babel. The disciples at Pentecost made a name not for themselves, but for God. 'In our own languages we hear them speaking of God's acts of power,' the book of Acts records. Those earliest disciples were dead to their own glory, and fascinated by the glory of God. Because God is acknowledged as all-powerful, communication between human beings can at last take place.

The glory of God, of course, can be seen in Europe's secular developments. There are the many scientific and educational advances since the Age of the Enlightenment, the advances in technology, and the developments of reason. But if Europe seeks to forget God, and does not also inherit and survive with the great values of its Judaeo-Christian tradition, it falls into anguish, because it fails to look beyond herself. One of the main tasks of the Church must be, then, to act as the repository of the continent's tradition, not by resorting to simplistic answers or a stance of opposition and rejection, but by recalling Europe to its roots in God, the God who in his dying and rising for us showed us the dignity of the human person and the transcendent meaning of human relationships. It is this which has shaped the way Europe celebrates its great mysteries of living and dying; it is this which has given Europe its grand projects – its soul; its heart; its true vocation.

The then Cardinal Ratzinger once wrote:

> the Church, or Churches, should first of all truly be themselves. Christians must not allow themselves to be downgraded to a mere means for making society moral, as the liberal State wished; still less should they want to justify themselves through the usefulness of their social works. The more the Church understands herself, first and foremost as the institute for social progress, the more the social vocations dry up – the calls to serve the old, the sick, children – vocations that flourished so much when the Church still looked essentially to God.

It is the proof of Jesus's words 'seek first the Kingdom of God and his righteousness and all the rest will be given you' (Mt. 6). What the Church must first do, decisively, is what is her very own: she must fulfil the task to which her identity is based, to make God known and to proclaim His Kingdom. (*Turning Point for Europe?* pp. 173-4)

In response, therefore, to many of the challenges posed by developments in science, technology, communication, and political conflict, the Church's primary task is to fulfil the purpose for which the Holy Spirit was poured out on us – to proclaim Jesus Christ. The Pentecost narrative tells us what that proclamation must be like: not based on words or human wisdom, but on the Spirit and on his power. It must start with the *kerygma* – the proclamation of the death and resurrection of Jesus Christ – and only then lead people into the *didache*, the moral teaching and the law. The proclamation of Christ is the ploughshare that opens up the furrow in the earth to receive the seeds for future sowing. That is how it was in the beginning of the Church, and how it must be again today if we are to re-evangelise Europe.

That is why the Church, faced with the innumerable challenges and questions posed by modern technology and progress, should not be tempted into a fundamentalist rejection of modern attitudes or trapped in single issues. Many people identify the Church and its message primarily with issues concerning gender and sexual ethics. But we have to show that the Church's response is of sufficient complexity to offer our creative answers and comments on difficult questions, rooting our answers always in our concern for what I call 'cherishing life'. These include, of course, issues of sexual morality and genetics; but also issues of world trade, the ecological dimension of our stewardship of the planet, global poverty and solidarity, how to make peace in situations of conflict. For these are all questions rooted in the duty of love. The Church's teaching in these areas must always be an invitation to real happiness and to a discipleship rooted in the true meaning of love. Failure to love is the greatest sin. Making known the love of God poured out for humankind is our work, and our calling. When we fail to persuade through statements which are purely authoritative, we must remember that we are converted by witnesses to that love rather than by words.

That great twentieth-century theologian Karl Rahner was right, therefore, in his apparently extreme statement that 'the Christian of tomorrow will be a mystic or he will not be at all'. The full life to which the Church must now invite Europe, as never before, is a life which includes the centrality of the interior life, both individually and in community.

The Church must learn better to witness to true freedom by linking it to solidarity. We are most free when we are entangled in healthy relationships with others, not when we are lone rangers. Contemporary Europe has enabled, on one level, a hitherto unheard-of liberty – politically, socially, economically. Our TV remote control caters for the twitchiest viewer; the Internet is a marvellous instrument for retrieving information immediately from a dazzling array of sources; Easyjet and Ryanair take us anywhere in Europe for the price of a train ticket; the mobile phone enables us to make plans and to keep changing them as circumstances change. These are great developments, which are causing a significant change in our mindsets, just as, in the late nineteenth century, rapid developments in industrial production led to huge social mobility and change. But technology must be our servant, not our master; we must shape it to God-shaped human priorities, not the other way round. In the Victorian era our factories caused us to see people as less than human, as factors in production, and this corrosion led, indirectly, to mass politics and totalitarianism, to the extinction of our freedom. Today the extension of choice to all sectors of human life is corroding our consciences in the same way. People are as good as their contracts, to be hired and fired at will; relationships become transitory, ad hoc, dispensable; old people and immigrants are diminished in the eyes of society, scapegoated as parasitic or useless; we wish to create human beings for particular purposes, not receive them as gifts. All these are challenges to our freedom, because they lock us in ourselves and create vicious circles of anger and rejection and violence.

The Church's reasoned arguments must always witness to true freedom, the kind of freedom that comes with an acknowledgement that God created the world and each of us, and that the meaning of life starts from that reeling truth. We must learn how to show that the Church's moral doctrines are not what secular Europe so often reduces them to – a manual of dos and don'ts – but, rather, an invaluable guide on how to be truly human.

The truth, Jesus said, will make us free; the truth is for everyone, equally, and it starts from a Creator God for whom we are all – all of us – 'worth it'. When the truth becomes 'my' truth, something valid for me but for no one else, against which only I can be judged, then it ceases to be truth; it becomes a prison of untruth in which I am locked away, unable to reach out to others. The contrast between Babel and Pentecost is again instructive, here. They are like two building sites, in which two cities are under construction – an idea which St Augustine took up in his *City of God*. The city of Babel, founded on love of self taken to the extreme of despising God, and the City of God, founded on the love of God to the extreme of surrendering our egos. Each of us is called to choose which of the two building sites we wish to work on.

There are many aspects of modern Europe which are Babel-like, and they can be seen most clearly in the breakdown of communities. From earliest times, the centrality of the community has been part of the essential shape of the Church. The Church must be seen to be creatively building community by valuing the resources and gifts of all, and especially, as l'Arche shows us, those of the ones most despised by society. In our Church it means valuing the resources of all, including lay people, and especially women, for the building up of our ecclesial communities. John Paul himself said so in his document on the dignity of women, *Mulieris Dignitatem*. We have yet to make its insights, like so much of his wisdom, our own.

The theologians teach us that the *pleroma*, the fullness of graces and gifts, is to be found in the Church. But we need to believe that and to implement it, to persuade each individual believer that we need his and her gifts in order to enjoy that fullness. The hoped-for recognition of the gifts of all lay men and women in our Church will never be realised until we embrace the reawakening of the charisms in our time.

And this must be true, too, of the universal Church. The word for it is *koinonia* – communion. It is, in many ways, *the* way in which the Church understands and expresses herself since the Second Vatican Council. Pope John Paul in his Apostolic Letter, 'At the Beginning of the Second Millennium', challenges us to give new momentum to an ecclesiology of communion. There is much still to be done in strengthening communion within the governance of the Church. In the Acts of the Apostles, Peter never acts alone: Peter stands with the eleven – the model from which today we get the model of the Pope governing with the bishops. My weeks in Rome, spent discussing the Church in the world in the company of my brother bishops, were a wonderful experience of that collegiality, which many are calling at this time to be strengthened. And I have every confidence that it will be, as Pope Benedict XVI signalled in his address to the cardinals when he asked 'my brothers in the Episcopate to be close to me in prayer and to counsel so that I may be truly the servant of the servants of God'.

When the Church lives, in the core of its being, the Trinitarian value of communion, it provides the energy and the inspiration for the creation of authentic communities in our society. Our pastoral planning must make it easier for people to nurture their interior life when they come through our doors, to find beyond them places of welcome. This is what amazed the five young men who went to Worth Abbey to take part in a three-part television programme, called *The Monastery*, documenting a six-week experiment in monastic living. Many of you will have seen the final part last night. These young men – a snapshot of our contemporary Europeans – were overwhelmed by the sense of being accepted for who they were, yet at the same time grateful to be challenged to be much more than who they were, to be offered, without apology, the gospel which those monks are living out with dedication. Their guests had different responses to that gift, but all were in some way changed by it.

Fifty years ago I read a book which transformed my thinking about the role of small communities in the life of the Church. It was by an eminent theologian, the Dominican Yves Congar. In one part of the book he speaks about the communal, or community life, of the Church. He speaks particularly about the need for small communities, how many people re-discover the Church, not from above, namely the hierarchy or the priests, but rather from below. He says,

> Many of our contemporaries find that for them the Church's machinery, sometimes the very institution, is a barrier obscuring her deep and living mystery which they can find or find again only from below, through little church cells, wherein the mystery is lived directly and with great simplicity . . . A need is felt to seek beneath the readymade administrative machinery, the living reality of basic communities, the aspect in which the Church herself is at the same time as an objective institution or hierarchical mediation, a community, to whose life all its members contribute and is patterned by a give and take and a pooling of resources. (*Lay People in the Church*, p. 324)

I believe that some form of community life is more and more necessary for many Christians in today's Europe. No one can be a Christian alone. He or she needs to be part, not only of the parish community, but also of a more intimate community which supports and nourishes their faith. Prayer, community and service to others are the hallmark of the Christian life. The Church must offer these; parishes need to make them easily accessible – an opportunity for prayer, community life, as well as service to those less fortunate in society or in the world. This will mean – as has already happened – that our parish structure will have to become more flexible. People will seek on a Sunday to join a particular celebration of the Holy Eucharist with a substantial number of other Catholics and, with them, form a living, worshipping community. In the big European cities such as London, people are seeking, alongside and usually within their parish, a more intense experience of faith community of the sort that many movements offer – meeting weekly, or less often, to grow in discipleship. Faith-sharing groups, of the sort that have developed in my diocese with the programme of *At Your Word Lord*, where 20,000 people have been meeting weekly across parishes in Westminster, need to become a normal fact of our daily church life. Prayer circles, Scripture-reading groups, retreats – these need to be the daily bread which nourishes us, in order to nourish others.

Our new shape must allow people to learn freedom through solidarity. Solidarity, first, with the despised of our communities – with the less-abled and the elderly, with immigrants and refugees, with the hungry and the lonely and the imprisoned. And solidarity, too, with those we do not know, but who are no less our brothers and sisters in Christ across the developing world. The contemporary European seeker wants to see the Kingdom of God being lived; he or she wants to know what a difference the gospel makes. So many people meet Jesus Christ every day in the helpless and vulnerable, learning from them what it is to be human. I would like every Catholic to think about the way he or she can give some time each week to crossing a boundary of fear in society, and befriending those on the other side, and to be bold in witnessing to the gift of the poor to us all.

The men who took part in *The Monastery* were agnostic, or at least uncommitted, and in some cases deeply sceptical. Yet, as I said, they were grateful to be challenged. They have been left empty by the constant pursuit of gratification, of the avoidance of a confrontation with the inevitability of death. More than one of the participants met all the requirements of secular Europe for a happy and fulfilled life – success, good looks, youth, energy, endless choice – yet these had left them with a nagging sense that this was a lie, that true happiness lay elsewhere. Some showed strong signs of despair.

The modern European, despite – or perhaps because of – great liberties, is in many ways a person of angst. Our new Pope, in his book *The Salt of the Earth*, speaks about 'a struggle between love and a refusal to love'. He goes on to define the role of the Church in relation to human history as being 'to offer the world an escape from itself into the

89

light of God and to keep open this possibility so that the air we breathe can penetrate into the world'. This challenge, it seems to me, underlies all the different challenges which I have outlined. It is essentially a spiritual one, and it must be one that the Church must be confident in offering an answer to.

One of the great paradoxes of our age is that religion is considered by many to be boring, yet religion is concerned with matters too dramatic to be put – except rarely, as in the case of *The Monastery* – on stage and on screen. It is, in fact, the greatest spiritual writers and theologians who have understood the real drama, which is why they have always tried to shake us out of our complacency, to wake us up to what is really going on under the surface of our lives. The Italian Archbishop, Bruno Forte, a contemporary theologian, makes this point well when he says:

> Choice is urgent and decisive – between living like pilgrims in search of the hidden countenance, letting ourselves be guided by the fatherly-motherly hand of the Other, or shutting ourselves in our fears and our loneliness. Life is either a pilgrimage or a foretaste of death. It is either passion, search and restlessness, or it is letting ourselves die a little each day, escaping in all the ways our society makes possible and that help us be distracted and not ask the real questions. A decision must be made. I will arise and go to my father, said the Prodigal Son. We have to open ourselves, to listen and to cry out. This is the most necessary choice for our women and men of this post-modern age. (*The Essence of Christianity*, pp. 12-13)

I remember watching a film, years ago, called *Brother Sun, Sister Moon*. In it, St Francis answers before the bishop as he is confronted by his father, who asks him to give back money he has given away. So, Francis strips himself naked before the bishop and says, 'Now I have no father but my Father who is in heaven.' And the bishop puts his cloak around him and he walks away. Only by dying to oneself can one rise to new life.

So, too, the Church dies and rises. 'Still doomed to death, and fated not to die,' wrote John Dryden, of the Church in England, three centuries ago. So we should not be surprised if the Church in her pilgrimage through history exhibits the dying and rising of her Master. Did she not die in those early centuries in the Catacombs and through those early persecutions – 'The blood of the martyrs is the seed of the Church,' said Tertullian – and rise again with Constantine? Did she not die in the Dark Ages and rise again with the monastic tradition and with those holy men and women, Dominic, Francis, Clare? And so it goes on. It once seemed impossible to the Church that the papacy could be exercised without the papal states. Yet the experience of the last 150 years is that their loss immeasurably increased the freedom and authority of the papacy. Never in history has there been a series of popes of the calibre of those we had in the twentieth century – and continuing, now, into the twenty-first century, with our new Pope, Benedict XVI.

In some ways the Church in Europe and, in particular, the Church in Britain is at such a time now. It is a time of dying and of rising. It is a time of crisis. By that word 'crisis', I do not mean a crisis of fear or of disintegration, but rather the New Testament understanding of crisis as a time of decision, a time of uncertainty, yes, but a time of change and development. We live in a rather strange, twilight time. We should not be surprised at the challenges and the nervousness and the fears that face us here in our own country as we look to the future and the shape of the Church to come.

Part of the Church's task now, therefore, is to offer people a real choice, a choice about salvation: pilgrimage or death. Babel or Pentecost. Despair or happiness. The challenge is to die, and to be reborn. The Church in its history can only repeat, in a mystical sense, the history of her divine Master. Jesus won for us our salvation and the promise of eternal life by his life, by his death on the cross, and by his resurrection. The Church lives again and again this truth – a hundred deaths, and a hundred resurrections. This means that we should not fear or be afraid as we face uncertainty and change, dying and rising.

Perhaps the greatest temptation in contemporary Europe is not great evil but indifference. 'Our age is an age of moderate virtue and of moderate vice,' says T.S. Eliot in *The*

Rock, 'when men will not lay down the Cross because they will never assume it.'

Some time ago I met the Archbishop of Prague, Cardinal Vlk, and during the meal we had together, he told me about his experiences during the Communist era in Czechoslovakia. He told me how, for ten years of his life, he was persecuted by the authorities and his licence to practise as a priest was removed. He was thrown out of his parish and told to earn his keep and make his own hidden way in the world. He became a window-cleaner in the city of Prague. One day he was cleaning windows. He was high up on a ladder on one of Prague's beautiful streets. Below was a group of German tourists window-shopping. He could hear them laughing, joking, and chatting about what they wanted to buy. And then it struck him. A voice deep within him: 'Nobody knows who you are . . . nobody cares that you are a priest, nobody cares that you have faith, nobody is interested in the message of Jesus that you preach.' He shared with me his sense of abandonment and isolation. But then he said, very beautifully and very pro-foundly, 'It became clear to me that the cross is not a pious object out there but the cross is a living reality in my life, for on the cross God is present but hidden.' His story reminded me that we all called in a very real way in our own humdrum lives to share in the cross, in the suffering of Jesus in our world today. We are called especially to search for the God who lies hidden in human suffering.

We are so often like the disciples on the road to Emmaus, focused on what appears to be receding, not on where we are going. In our twilight zone, it is easy to mistake thorns for flowers, and vice versa. But it is by dying that we live, as nature teaches us, as Golgotha teaches us, as John Paul – whose death has already brought many fruits – taught us.

And we must be willing, now, to allow ourselves little deaths in translating the gospel into pastoral initiatives adapted to the circumstances of our community, as Pope John Paul exhorted us to in *Novo Millennio Ineunte*. But if you were to say to me, 'What is the greatest priority for the Church in Europe at this time?' I would say quite simply this: that people should be invited ever more urgently to seek holiness. It begins in the family where children are taught how to pray by the example of their mother and/or father. It means people are helped to pray, encouraged to pray. There can be no Christian life without humbly turning to God in prayer. What nourishes this prayer is the example and invitation of Jesus himself. Every person by their baptism enters into the holiness of God, through being united with Christ and through the indwelling of his Holy Spirit. No baptised Christian should settle for a life of mediocrity.

I have seen in this Diocese how people have been changed and turned by reading the Scripture together and hearing together the voice of the Lord calling them to pray, to serve, to understand his way of life. I know that there are many who not only are invited to be holy but respond to that invitation day by day, year by year. Faith is nurtured by prayer. It is faith in the Risen Christ that sustains us through the trials and tribulations of life, but also animates us to give an example to Jesus by the way we live.

We pray at the Mass to God to 'protect us from all anxiety'. People may worry about the shortage of priests or the shortage of numbers or the difficulties that face us with the stagnation of belief and secularism of our country. We cannot, alone, solve these difficulties; but we can offer Jesus Christ crucified, and the power of the Holy Spirit to transform hearts. At one of our meetings in Rome an African Cardinal spoke of the appalling difficulties in his country, of aggressive Islam, the devastation of AIDS, the wars in his country, and its poverty. But then he said, 'I remember, in the Acts of the Apostles, Peter going towards the temple and a poor lame man asked them for help, for support. And Peter said, "Silver and gold I have not, but what I have I will give you. In the Name of Jesus Christ, stand up".'

This is why I feel full of confidence and hope for the Church in Europe as we face the future. The Church is alive – and on pilgrimage – as it has been for 2,000 years, as I saw so vividly out on that balcony above that roaring throng in St Peter's Square just a few weeks ago. What we have to offer is no less than Jesus Christ. It is a task which, carried out well, will recall Europe to its eternal destiny – to the life, meaning and hope for which our continent yearns.

'People are living in alienation, in the salt waters of suffering and death, in a sea of darkness without light,' Pope Benedict said at his inaugural Mass. 'The net of the Gospel pulls us out of the waters of death and brings us into the splendour of God's light – into true life,' he added. This is the purpose of the Church. This is our purpose. It is an awesome, and wonderful, task, to help Europe to be itself once more, to relive its roots, to discover its soul. And we are secure in the knowledge that God never fails us. Only when God is glimpsed does life truly start. Europeans are in need, as never before, of seeing God. We are the ones, with the help of God's grace, entrusted with revealing him.